ANGIE & MARIA

A Love Story

S. J. Lieberman

Lulu.com

ISBN 978-1-67814-832-4

Dedicated to the World War II Rosies.

CHAPTERS

The Bump .. 1
The Meeting .. 4
The Automat .. 9
Eighth Avenue .. 13
Apartment 4B .. 20
Mr. Berski .. 38
The Mentor .. 46
Times Square .. 55
The Gift .. 61
The Surrogates .. 64
Hello Joey! .. 66
Grow Up!! .. 72
Second Fiddle .. 77
Epilogue .. 84
Appendix .. 99

The Bump

It was Wednesday, October 28, 1963. Angie and Maria stood embraced arm-in-arm on 33rd Street to witness and mourn the demolition of New York Penn Station across the street. They had stopped by the previous week for a final nostalgic visit. Now jackhammers chipped away at the magnificent Beaux-Arts facade. The cacophonous destruction that assaulted their senses failed to chip away the shared memory of how their lives together began there on a Sunday, the fifth day of July 1942.

The United States had entered World War II right after the Japanese attack on Pearl Harbor the previous December. The Pacific war had begun to turn in America's favor after the decisive defeat of the Japanese carrier force at Midway a month earlier. Optimism for the war's outcome prevailed.

Hundreds of recruits arrived to report for Navy duty. Twenty-three-year-old newlyweds Angie and Bill caressed within a sea of eager recruits and their somber families and friends. From their dress, they appeared to be a middle-class couple who survived the Depression okay. Bill, a recently graduated civil engineer, volunteered for the Seabees. They've been a couple since high school and during their college years – never dated anyone else.

The large clock above the cavernous concourse indicated 11:36. It ticked off another minute – 11:37. Angie trembled as she watched another minute of her perfect life disappear.

Bill was handsomely tall with broad shoulders that hinted at an athletic physique under his light jacket. Angie was petite with raven hair, a flawlessly pale complexion, and dark eyes that blended into captivating beauty that epitomized the best her combined Italian-Scandinavian heritage could offer. Tearful eyes failed to hide her acute anxiety. Bill sensed her trembling. He hugged her even tighter, planted a gentle kiss on her forehead, pointed to the benches, and whispered. "Let's grab a seat over there."

She nodded.

Maria and Mateo, a young Puerto Rican couple, entered the concourse. They were about twenty or so, swarthy, black hair. Maria, a very attractive blue-eyed *Morenita*, a little taller than Angie, wore a slightly faded cotton dress. Mateo, a wiry dude, wore an old black gang-style leather jacket. *Why did he wear that thing in July?*

Bill bumped into them as they passed by. Maria stumbled, was almost knocked over. She dropped her small handbag. Some small items spilled out.

Mateo grabbed her to prevent her from falling. "*¿Estás bien?*"

She waved him off. "*¡Sí, no soy tan delicada. No te preocupes tanto!*"

Mateo, truculent, approached Bill. "Watch the hell where you goin', *pendejo.*"

Pen-day-ho? What the hell does that even mean? Who cares? Bill thrust his open palm toward him. This punk didn't intimidate him. "Chill! You don't wanna mess with me!" Mateo considered Bill's imposing stature and had the good sense to stop his approach. "Yeah, yeah! We good?"

"Yeah, we…we're good," said Bill.

Bill turned toward Maria and held out his hands as an apologetic gesture. "I'm so sorry. Did I hurt you?" *Huh? White people almost never apologized to her.* Speechless, she could only squeeze one of his hands, smile and shake her head. She crouched to retrieve her scattered items. Angie crouched to help.

"Thanks," said Maria.

"Hey! It's the least I can do. It's *our* fault," said Angie handing Maria a small coin purse. Maria gripped the purse and Angie's hand with both of hers. They locked gazes, couldn't resist each other's stare, mesmerized. Maria's grip made Angie feel uneasy, but oddly, she didn't want her to let go either.

Maria was flustered. "*¡Lo siento!* Uh, I mean I'm sorry. Don't mean ta stare. Never met nobody so pretty. Wow!" Maria maintained her tight grip on the coin purse and Angie's hand. The girls continued to gaze at each other, mutually mesmerized by some sort of strange unspoken connection. *What's going on here*?

Angie tapped Maria's grip with her other hand. "Uh, thanks. Met? Ha! More like bumped? Whadaya say we try again later? You know, meet after they check in."

Maria released her lingering grasp, still mesmerized by Angie's beauty, by her kindness.

"Uh, check in?"

"The Navy, our guys are joining the Navy, right?"

"Oh yeah, yeah…the Navy. Yeah, I would like to meet with ya later. I really would."

Maria finally broke her stare. Angie smiled and gave her a thumbs-up. "Great! Then let's look for each other after the check in. Okay?"

Maria returned a thumbs-up. "Yeah, let's do that." They rose from their crouched positions after retrieving all the spilled items.

"By the way, I'm Angie."

"Maria…I'm Maria. Yeah, let's do that."

The two couples went off in different directions. The girls glanced back at each other, each with a Mona Lisa smile.

The Meeting

The large clock indicated 12:41.

Angie and Bill huddled together on a bench. She looked at the clock – another minute gone. That exacerbated her anxiety, her tears. Bill dabbed her eyes with a handkerchief. "What if you don't come back and I never get to give you a little Bill or little Angie?"

Bill kissed her forehead. "Shhh! Don't say that." She zipped two fingers across her lips as if to close them shut and kissed his cheek. Angie hugged him even tighter. She removed a small photo of their wedding portrait from his shirt pocket, kissed the reverse side, and left a lipstick print. Bill kissed it and replaced the photo in his pocket. "I'm so freaking terrified to be alone without you, to go home to an empty apartment, to spend night after night without you next to me." Suddenly losing what was left of her composure, Angie bawled. Bill wiped her tears and planted gentle kisses on her head.

"It's war, honey. We all have to adjust. I'm sure you'll find a way."

"You think so, huh?"

"I know so. Growing up together I learned you're a lot tougher than you think." Angie broke their huddle. Her tear-filled eyes looked straight at him. "Oh yeah? Look at me. Do I look so tough right now?"

Angie and Bill huddled together again. They sat quietly for a while watching the crowd mill about.

"Hey, here's an idea," he said pointing to the crowd. "I bet there's a gal out there about your age who might be interested to move in with you so you won't be alone."

Angie considered his suggestion. "You think?"

Her positive response surprised and delighted him. "Why not? I bet you can find someone just like that. Maybe even someone who shares your interests." Angie's mood perked up as she thought back how the feeling, that strange but good feeling, felt when she and Maria gazed at each other.

"Yeah, maybe you're right. I think something clicked with that Spanish gal while I was helping to pick up her stuff. We agreed to get together."

Angie's upbeat mood delighted Bill even more. "Oh yeah? Great! Go for it. She might be just the ticket, might turn out to be a great roommate." Angie stepped onto the bench and scanned the crowd.

"See her?" asked Bill.

Disappointed, Angie shook her head.

*****

The large clock indicated 1:10.

Bill embraced Angie from behind as they stood watching the crowd mill about. He pulled aside her hair, exposed her neck, nuzzled, and kissed her. That never failed to erotically arouse Angie. She reached down behind herself and touched him. "Oh my," she exclaimed. Smiling impishly, Angie winked, pointed, and nodded toward the restroom area. Bill took her hand and they scurried there. He looked inside the men's room and beckoned her to enter.

*****

The large clock indicated 1:25.

They rushed out of the restroom. Bill held open the door for another couple to rush in. Bill and Angie were back among the crowd looking quite disheveled while happily enjoying their erotic afterglow. He stroked her hair to straighten it. She did the same for him.

*****

The large clock indicated 2:05.

Recruits gathered near a large poster that stated where they should assemble at 1400 hours. Angie and Bill hugged and kissed as did many other couples.

A Navy officer stood on a chair shouting through a cone-style megaphone. "Okay, guys. Listen up. When I call your name go to the check-in table over here." He pointed to the nearby table where sat a couple of petty officers. "When you hear your name, raise your hand and shout *here* or *yo* or anything else. You got a minute, just a minute, to say your good-byes. After you're checked off, go down those stairs to track three."

Angie and Bill continued to hug and kiss while names were called followed by *here* and *yo* responses.

"Ricci, William," shouted the Navy officer.

"Guess they didn't forget about me." He raised his hand. "Here!"

Angie and Bill hugged and passionately kissed for their allotted minute. They reluctantly released their embrace. Bill stepped to the check-in table. At the stairs, he turned for one last look at Angie and blew her a kiss. She returned her own kiss and waved until he disappeared into the gate.

Angie glanced at the large clock – 2:32. The last minute of her perfect life had just disappeared. *Please return…I need many millions more minutes.* Tears dripped down her cheeks.

The Navy officer continually called out recruit names. They responded with a *here* or *yo* or whatever. Angie took several deep calming breaths. Her mind cleared enough to remember her agreement to get together with that Spanish girl. She again stood on a bench and scanned the crowd.

Angie smiled through her tears when she spotted Maria hugging Mateo several yards away. She wistfully watched them. They were too far for her to hear them speak. Not important anyway, probably in Spanish. Angie noticed Mateo sneaking a small unidentifiable object from his jacket pocket into Maria's handbag.

"Torres, Mateo," shouted the Navy officer.

He hugged Maria with one arm and raised his other. "Yo!" They reluctantly ended their minute of hugging and kissing. Mateo stepped to the check-in table. He took one last look at Maria, blew her a kiss, pointed to her, and shouted. "*¡Recuerda, siempre te amaré!*" Maria nodded and waved back. She looked sad, but oddly, was dry-eyed. Maria watched him disappear down the stairs into the gate. Angie approached her from behind and tapped her shoulder. Maria flinched and spun around. Light-blue eyes contrasting with her swarthy scowl combined into a blood-chilling glower. *Oh my! You don't want to be on this chica's bad side!*

Angie recoiled, stuttered. "I, I, I, I'm Angie. Remember me?"

Maria's glower instantly changed to pleasant recognition then remorse. *"¡Madre mía! ¡Madre mía!* I didn't mean to scare ya. I get jumpy when someone sneaks up on me from behind especially if I dunno know who it is. Please forgive me."

"What's wrong with me? First we crash into you and almost knock you over. Now I sneak up on you. No, *you* should forgive me."

The two girls locked gazes as before, again mutually mesmerized by that strange unspoken connection. *What's going on here?*

"Oh, uh! You kidding me? How can anyone *ever* forget your pretty face?"

"Uh, Bill just left for the service too. I was watching you and Mateo. Heard his name called by the Navy guy."

They stared at each other. Neither knew what to say next. Angie broke the awkward silence.

"Uh, would you like to get something to eat? My treat."

"Oh c'mon. That ain't right. We just met. You wanna treat someone like me?"

Maria's remark puzzled Angie. They momentarily just stared at each other.

"No, no, no! Shouldn'ta said that!" apologized Maria.

"Uh, people sometimes, you know, sometimes become friends even after they *just met*."

Maria gave her an incredulous look.

Is this chick for real? Maria instinctively kept up her guard with white people. But this chick, no, this lady, this white lady seemed so…seemed so devoid of guile. She could not not accept Angie's invitation.

"Something wrong?"

Maria shook her head. *"¡Madre mía!* You're *so* nice!" Angie smiled and grasped her hand. Maria guardedly smiled at her. "There's an Automat couple of blocks over on Eighth," said Angie.

The Automat

Angie and Maria placed their dishes on a table and stacked the empty trays aside. Silent smiles flitted between them as they ate. "Where do you live?" asked Angie eager to end the awkward silence.

"Bronx, South Bronx, with my folks and little brother."

"How about that? I used to live in the Bronx too before Bill and I got married and moved to Queens."

"Where in the Bronx?"

"Near the Pelham Bay Sound View station."

"Oh yeah? I live near the Hunts Point station." Maria mentally named and counted station stops. *Whitlock, Elder, Soundview*. "That's just three stations apart."

"How about that? Only a five-minute train ride," replied Angie.

"Close, but a world apart."

"Whadaya mean?"

"South Bronx is a tough Latino neighborhood. What was yours like?"

"Nice area. Mostly Jewish and Italian. Bill's grand folks and Dad's folks came from Italy."

"Angie short for somethin'?"

"Yeah, Angelina. Used to be Angelina Coiro before Bill made me Angelina Ricci."

Maria stared at her with wary, narrowed eyes.

Maria's look puzzled Angie. "Something wrong?"

Maria shook her head. "Angelina. Angelina. That sounds so pretty, so classy. Just like you."

"Thanks. You're very kind."

Maria's fear about trusting *white* people began to fade, at least with this person who sat across from her. *This Angie person seems to be the real deal…better check her out some more to be sure.*

"Where'd ya go to school?"

"P.S. 77, James Monroe High, City College," replied Angie. "How about you?"

"Saint Joseph Elementary and South Bronx High. I took some bookkeeping classes. I get some part-time work doin' that. What did ya learn about in college?"

"Me to be an English teacher. Bill to be a civil engineer. That's why he enlisted for the Seabees."

"I was pretty good in math," said Maria. "Wish I could go t'college but my folks need me t'help out financially."

The girls finished their meals in silence. Smiles flitted between them. Not so awkward anymore.

"How'd y'meet Bill?"

"I had a crush on him in high school. He would sneak looks at me, but too shy to come over. Mom showed me how to get him to talk to me. This was in the tenth grade, both fifteen years old, you know. He always gave me a smile, good looking boy, really nice, not silly like other boys. I think he really wanted to talk to me but couldn't seem to get up the nerve. He was always polite. I really wanted to talk to him."

"So how'd ya get to do that?"

"I asked Mom for advice. She said girls are sick and tired of waiting for boys to do the asking. If you *really* like him, she said, *you* do the asking. Go right up to him and say *Hi, Bill, I'm Angie!* He'll probably be shocked you know his name. Ask him what his interests are. She reminded me to keep eye contact, smile, and just listen. Also to gently stroke the back of his hand while you just listen. That's very important, she said. That's all it took for Dad to fall in love with her."

"Really? That simple?"

"Yup! Kind of sneaky, I know. But I *really* wanted to get his attention. It also didn't hurt that Mom is also very beautiful." Angie removed a wallet, with some family photos, from her handbag. She showed Maria her mother's picture in a ballet costume.

"Your mom is a ballerina?"

"Yeah, when she was younger. Isn't she beautiful? I really lucked out having gorgeous parents. This is a picture of my dad."

"Ah! Now I see why you're so pretty."

"She taught me some ballet. I didn't care for it, really tough on the feet. But four years ago our folks treated us to Benny Goodman's Carnegie Hall concert. Bill and I learned to swing dance after that. We just love, love, love to swing dance, every chance we could get."

"Yeah, me too. But back to how you met Bill. Did you follow your mom's advice?"

"I did! I got up some courage one day and did. Mom was right. Turns out he was good at science and math. I was so-so with those subjects. He tutored me throughout high school and college. I became his only girlfriend, *ever*. He became my only boyfriend, *ever*. We only had eyes for each other…Jeez, I miss him so much," she said finger wiping her eyes.

"That is such a nice story!"

"Okay, your turn. How'd you meet Mateo?"

"Nothing shy about Mateo. Scoped me in the Barrio one day. Comes right up ta me all macho, real cool like. We talked, went for a Coke and little over a month later I became Navy bride Maria Torres. No more Maria Garcia. Got hitched last Tuesday at the courthouse…Every girl's dream wedding, right? Yeah, I know. Too soon. Me nineteen, him twenty-two. He insisted so I get benefits."

The girls finished their meals.

"Do you have more time to talk?" asked Angie.

"Yeah, sure. It's Sunday. No need to do anything special now. I can go back home anytime. And besides, I like talkin' with you. You're nice, real nice. I don't know many people like you who wanna talk to someone like me."

Maria's remark shocked and puzzled Angie. "I don't know what that means. You have to tell me what you mean."

Maria squirmed in her seat and hesitated to answer. She looked nervous trying to change the subject. "Uh, ya mind talkin' outside? I feel like walking if ya don't mind."

"No, no. I don't mind at all. I like to walk too. Besides," said Angie wiping her eyes, "I have only an empty apartment to go to now."

The girls picked up their handbags and exited the Automat onto Eighth Avenue.

Eighth Avenue

They strolled up Eighth Avenue, silent for a while.
"I'm sorry, I didn't mean t'say that," said Maria breaking the silence.

"But you *did* say it. You wouldn't have if something wasn't bothering you." They stopped walking. Maria looked right into Angie's eyes. "Honest? You really wanna know what's bugging me?"

"I know we just met, but yes. I really do. I really wanna know."

Maria once again stalled and hesitated to explain. *That was it! In Maria's mind this woman really was the real deal.* She started to hook her arm into Angie's arm. "Is it okay for me to do this?"

"Yes, of course!"

The girls continued their arm-in-arm stroll up Eighth Avenue, silent for a while.

"This is the heart of the Garment District. Kind of eerie being so empty on Sunday for such a busy place during the week," said Angie trying anything to rekindle the conversation.

"Yeah, I know. *Mamá* is a seamstress here," said Maria. They continued strolling up Eighth Avenue, again silent for a while.

"Look, if you don't wanna tell me what's bothering you, that's fine. It's none of my business anyway," said Angie.

Their conversation was interrupted as two matronly women approached chatting in Italian. Those shapeless black dresses they wore amused Maria. *What is it with these black dresses? Some kind of old country mourning uniform? Let it go, already! You're in America!*

The chatter stopped as they got closer to the girls. They sneered at Maria. She fixated her glower at them, stiff armed, and muttered as they came within earshot. "Fongool!"

The two alarmed Italian women hastened past the girls.

"How do you know that word?" asked Angie, a bit surprised.

"I know stuff. Y'see the look them freakin' bitches gimmee? Same look throwin' insults at *Mamá* because she's *Puertorriqueña*. Why can't they give *Mamá* just a little respect?"

Angie suddenly realized why her Italian name unsettled this Puerto Rican girl. They continued their arm-in-arm stroll, again silent for a while. Angie gazed at Maria with amused admiration. "I like you, Maria. I really like you."

"How come?"

"Jeez! I dunno. It's a feeling that's hard to explain. All I know for sure is that I get a really good feeling about you. Kinda like I wanna get to know you better. Do *you* like me?"

Maria's eyes misted over, almost on the verge of tears. They stopped strolling. Angie broke their arm-in-arm hold and looked directly into Maria's eyes. Angie became more impatient with Maria's reluctance to say what was bothering her. "Okay. Enough is enough. I swear, it's like pulling teeth. I'm not leaving until you tell me what's going on with you."

The two girls stood facing each other on the almost empty street.

Maria's resistance was finally broken. "Okay! Okay! Back at Penn Station ya gave me this wonderful warm feeling. Like somethin' never in my whole life. Yeah, you're freakin' pretty, but that's not it. It's the *way* y'looked at me! Here you are, a beautiful college-educated white lady not disgusted lookin' at a spic, a brown-skinned spic! Like them two bitches gimmee."

"A what? What the hell does your skin color have to do with anything?"

Maria raised her voice. "A *spic*! A brown-skinned *spic*! Should all go back to Puerto Rico with their gangs and drugs. We're not *all* like that, dammit!"

Angie stood speechless staring at Maria, a very angry Maria. "I'm from the tough Spanish South Bronx. You're from a *nice* Italian-Jewish area, or so ya tell me. Let me

tell you somethin' about your *nice* Italians and Jews.
There's lotsa Italian and Jewish immigrant seamstresses
in the Garment District. Ya got no idea the kinda shit
Mamá gotta put up with the insults from her *nice* Italian
and Jewish coworkers just so she can earn a little money."

Maria's demeanor elevated to seething anger. "And
don't get me started on those freakin' bastards who run
those freakin' garment factories now with the freakin'
craziness to make those freakin' Army and Navy
uniforms." She paused to take a few breaths, calmed
down, and looked at Angie standing there stunned and
speechless.

"Now here you are, an Italian white lady who *really*
cares what's goin' on with this spic. I'm not used to that,
Angie. That's what ya wanted to know, right?" Angie
cautiously reached for Maria's shoulder, hesitated to
touch. "Is this okay?"

"Yeah, yeah, sure." Angie's gentle touch brought Maria
to tears. Angie took a handkerchief from her handbag
and dabbed Maria's eyes.

"Thanks." Maria sniffled. "Wanna know why I'm
crying?"

Angie nodded.

"The only, really the *only* other white lady who cared
about me was Mrs. Butler, my bookkeeping and math
teacher. She was in her fifties, I think. I really missed her
after graduation."

"Wait, Maria." Angie pointed to a closed factory
building. "Let's go sit and talk on that stoop."

*****

They sat hip-to-hip on the stoop.

"Like I was sayin', Mrs. Butler would always take time
to listen to me. I can't forget how y'looked and gave me
that wonderful feeling. Don' wanna forget."

"Oh yeah? I have news for you, girl. You looking back at
me also gave me a warm fuzzy feeling. Something really
special. Like I really wanted you for my friend. Can't
explain it! Just something about you feels so right!"

Maria stared eyes widened at Angie. "How is that

possible? Italians and *Puertorriqueños* never get along."

"Listen to me! I'm a second-generation native-born American. My Italian name doesn't make me an Italian. I'm an American just like you. Kahpeesh?"

"But you got this pretty dress. Won't ya be embarrassed bein' seen with someone like me in this faded old thing?"

Angie stared at Maria for a brief moment. "What's with all the excuses? Don't you wanna be my friend?"

Maria stared incredulously at Angie. "You? A college-educated white lady actually wants someone like *me* for a friend?"

"Yes! Not just *a* friend. *My* friend! And stop saying *someone like me*. Give it a rest!"

"Y'really mean it? No bull?"

"No bull."

"You! *You* want *me* for a friend! No bull!"

"*My* friend! No bull. How many times I gotta say it?"

Maria's eyes welled up. Angie again dabbed her eyes. Maria sniffled. "Thanks. Mrs. Butler would always take time t'listen t'me, just like you're doin' right now. Wish we never met!"

"What? Why?"

"You're the only white lady who ever said she wants me for her friend. Betcha got no idea what that means t'me?"

The girls gazed at each other for a brief moment. "If we never met I wouldn' be losin' a wonderful friend when y'go back t'Queens." Maria hunched over, hugging herself, and sobbed. "I can't catch a freakin' break."

Angie again dabbed Maria's eyes and wrapped her arm around her shoulders. She waited for her to calm down. "Okay. My turn to talk. Okay?"

Maria sniffled, nodded.

"Let's get the skin color issue out of the way. Okay?"

Maria nodded.

"Dad has an Italian light caramel skin color, something like you, matter of fact."

"Wow! Never called caramel before."

"And Mom has a gorgeous Scandinavian pale complexion. Know what that makes me?"

Maria shook her head.

"Makes me a Latin and Nordic mixed-breed. A mongrel, a mutt. Thanks to Mom, I am, as you say, a *white lady*. A *white lady* mutt."

"But you're such a pretty mutt!"

Angie burst out laughing, but her laughter was immediately cut short by Maria's tears.

"What's wrong? I thought it was funny."

"You're goin' back t'Queens t'disappear from my life forever."

Angie wiped Maria's tears while recalling Bill's suggestion. *I bet there's a gal out there about your age who might be interested to move in with you so you won't be alone.*

She mentally prepared herself to offer a *quid pro quo* deal to this delightful Spanish girl she had only known for a few hours. Angie took a deep breath and steadied her nervousness for what she was about to do.

"Maybe not," said Angie.

"Huh?"

"Maybe I *don't* have to disappear from your life and at the same time maybe *you* can help me."

"How can *I* possibly help you?"

"Stick with me. Okay?"

"Yeah…Okay."

Angie took a couple of more deep breaths, still nervous. "Okay, here goes."

She took another deep breath. "I never lived alone my whole life. First with my folks as I grew up and then with Bill since we got married last month. Now with him away maybe for years, you have no idea how much living all alone worrying about him day and night scares me. I'm talking major league terrified!"

Angie paused. Maria stared at her waiting for her to continue.

"Uh, yeah. So since you're now married you might not wanna live with your folks any longer." She again inhaled a deep breath…slowly exhaled. "So how would you like to share my apartment with me while our guys are away?"

Maria stared at her in stunned silence.

"You're joking, right?"

"Joking? I'm scared out of my mind about being alone and you think I'm joking?"

Maria shook her head.

"Okay then. Whadaya think? We like each other, right?"

"Yeah. That's what I'm thinkin'. Won't your folks think you're nuts livin' with a South Bronx *chica* y'just met? Maybe in a gang?"

"Are you in a gang?"

"No, no, no! Never was a deb. I swear. Papi woulda kick me outa the house."

"Okay then. Yeah, probably will, but they'll be okay after I tell 'em about you and also about being a Navy wife too."

"Y'really sure about this?"

"I know it's just a gut feeling, but you feel..." Angie patted herself on her chest, "...you feel so right for me. Jeez, who wouldn't want you for her friend?" Maria's eyes welled up in disbelief of what she was hearing.

Angie again dabbed Maria's eyes. "I have a nice fold-out bed you can use. We can do stuff together like shopping and cooking and talking and seeing movies. We can also go into the city and swing dance at the USO. I think we can have fun together. Whadaya think?"

"What an offer! Dunno know how to answer that."

"Will you at least think about it?"

"Can't chip in much for rent or groceries. Don' have a steady job. Maybe spouse benefits can help a little."

"Not a problem. My real problem is I'm so scared to live alone. I have to pay the same rent with *or* without you. Don't worry about groceries. That's how you can help me. Your company would be priceless."

"Y'should know I'm a freakin' good cook."

"Oh yeah? What a deal! I'll get company and a chef."

"Just a cook. I ain't that fancy."

"I have a good paying job doing defense work at the Grumman factory in Bethpage. Maybe you can get one there too. They're always looking for all kinds of help."

"Full time?"

"Uh huh. Even provide training if they think you'd be good for something after an interview. They prefer women with family in the service and no kids to worry about at home because of possible overtime work."

"Gotta think. Need time t'think."

"Okay, then think about this. I live in a nice neighborhood. No gangs. No drugs. No crime. Wouldn't you like to get away from all that?"

Visions of the deteriorating South Bronx paraded through Maria's mind. She would be an idiot to pass on this offer. And Maria was no idiot!

She slapped herself on the forehead. That, of course, startled Angie. "That clinches it," proclaimed Maria.

Angie crossed fingers with her hand hidden from Maria's view. "Does that mean?"

Maria tossed her a big smile and enthusiastic nod.

"You make me so happy! When can you move in?"

"Not sure how my folks are gonna feel about their little girl movin' out, but let's see how it goes. I am *soooo* excited! Tomorrow evening okay?"

"Tomorrow? Really? Wow! That's great! Now you got me all excited too."

Angie took out a pencil and small notebook from her handbag. She turned to a blank page and wrote. "This is my address. Take the Lex, transfer at fifty-first. Get off at Forest Hills. It's just a few blocks from my place."

Angie kept writing. "This is the telephone number at Ziegler's candy store across the street. In case anything changes, leave a message and someone will put a note under my door." Angie tore out the notebook paper and handed it to Maria. "I get home from work about six. Wait in the candy store if you get there before that. I'll look for you there."

"How can I ever thank you?" They locked gazes. *They seemed to do that a lot.*

"Easy," said Angie. "Just show up."

Apartment 4B

The next day, Monday, late afternoon, Angie got off her bus from work. Mr. Ziegler, the candy store owner, spotted her through his plate glass store window. He rushed outside – shouted and waved for her to come over. *"Angie! Hey Angie!"* She turned and looked at him holding out her arms in a questioning gesture.

"Your friend, your friend Maria is here!"

Instantly excited, Angie looked both ways to avoid traffic and scurried across the street to the candy store. Mr. Ziegler held open the store door for her to rush in. Popular music played from the store radio with occasional news announcements about the war. Maria sat in one of the store booths. One small and two larger suitcases were on the floor next to her booth bench. Her small handbag was on the table. Sitting with her was her smiling father. Maria rose to greet Angie who ran to her with open arms. Angie's enthusiastic hug pleasantly surprised Maria.

"I am *so* happy to see you! I had a sleepless night. I was alone in bed worrying you wouldn't come."

"Well, here I am! This is my *Papi*, Vicente Garcia."

Sr. Garcia smiled warmly as he stood to greet Angie. He held out his hand to shake hers. Angie embraced his hand with her two hands. "What a nice surprise! I am so pleased to meet you, Mr. Garcia."

"Maria told so much wonderful things about you. I wanted to help with her suitcases and to meet you. But I must get back because I have a job to go to early tomorrow." He kissed Maria's cheek and whispered. *"Tenías razón. Ella es tan simpática y tan bonita también."*

"¿No te dije, Papi?" replied Maria.

Sr. Garcia smiled and waved to the girls as he left the candy store. They waved back. The girls sat back at the booth facing each other. They held hands across the table.

"Did I pass?" asked Angie.

"*And how!* Believe me, after my pitch yesterday a quick look and a hello was all he needed."

"Something to drink? An egg cream maybe?" Maria nodded with a smile. Angie turned to Mr. Ziegler holding up her two fingers. "Two egg creams, please." He acknowledged her order with a thumbs-up.

"So how did it go with your folks?"

"Complete surprise! Told 'em all aboutcha and your offer. They were thrilled t'death for me t'get outa the neighborhood. Couldn't help me fast enough t'pack my stuff. Even gave me fifty bucks t'chip in for rent and groceries. They really can't afford that. Gotta pay 'em back somehow."

"I told you that wasn't necessary."

"Yeah, I know. But they wouldn' let me mooch off your generosity." Angie gave Mr. Ziegler an appreciative nod as he served the egg creams. Silent smiles flitted between them as they sipped their drinks.

*****

The girls finished their drinks. Angie reached across the table and wiped some foam from Maria's lip. She wiped her own lip. "Okay, roomie, ready to go home?"

"Home. That sounds so nice. Yeah, I'd love to go home."

Angie paid Mr. Ziegler for the egg creams. She noticed a young guy through the plate glass window. He carried two large paper grocery bags in his brawny arms. Angie pointed toward him. "Do you know that guy across the street?"

"Yeah, that's Joey Collins."

"Why does he always hide his face?"

"Sad story. He was in the Merchant Marines. His convoy ship to Britain was torpedoed last September, face got burned really bad. Really nice kid, but very shy, especially around girls. Shame, only nineteen. His injury makes him even more shy. Ashamed to show his scars. Only comes out to shop for his family." He pointed through the plate glass window to an apartment building. "Joey lives over there with his mother and sister."

Maria proceeded out the store door with her two larger

suitcases and her handbag. Angie followed her with the small suitcase.

*****

The girls reached the front of Angie's apartment building. "Well, Maria, this is it!"

"Nice! Much nicer than my Bronx tenement."

Angie bumped open the building entrance door with her butt and held it open for Maria. They stepped to the elevator. Angie pressed the button and they watched the elevator floor level indicator reach the ground floor.

"Wow! This is a treat! I never lived with an elevator before! Just walk-ups."

"Nothing but the best for my roomie!"

The girls entered the elevator. Angie pressed the button for the fourth floor. A quiet hum from the elevator motor accompanied its rise.

Maria scanned the elevator walls, ceiling, floor, door, button panel like an amazed child, in this instance a nineteen-year-old amazed child with a new toy. Sure, she's been in department-store and office-building elevators. But an elevator where you live – Wow!

The elevator door opened. They stepped out and walked the hallway to apartment 4B. Angie reached into her handbag for her key, unlocked, and opened the door. With a smile and flourish, Angie ushered Maria inside. "Here we are, roomie! Home sweet home!"

The girls entered and placed the suitcases on the foyer floor. They proceeded to the kitchen with its typical items – kitchen table and chairs, plain cabinets, refrigerator, four-burner gas range with oven, sink with an adjoining drain board cover over the wash tub, small clock and radio on the counter. Angie placed Maria's handbag on the kitchen table.

"Oh, Angie! This is *so* nice! Such a treat! You never seem to stop giving me gifts! I'm not a strictly religious person, but some power brought you into my life."

"It's just one bedroom, a bathroom, a small living room. Here, let me show you around." Angie took Maria's hand and led her to the living room.

"*Oh my!* That is really nice furniture."

"Yeah. Our folks gave it to us for a wedding gift. They're so thrilled that Bill and I got married. They said it was our gift to them."

"Grand kids, huh?"

"Oh yeah! They'll have to wait for Bill to get back." Angie paused momentarily and sighed. "Anyway, the fold-out is your bed. They also gave us this nice Zenith record player because Bill..." Angie's eyes welled up. She wiped them with her fingers. "...because Bill and I love to dance." Angie pointed to the two hallway clothes closets. "I moved Bill's things into mine." Angie's eyes moistened again. "You must think I'm a big crybaby. Can't help it. I miss him so much." Maria gently touched Angie's shoulder. Angie smiled appreciatively at her for that kind gesture. "I moved Bill's things into mine so this one is now yours." Angie opened the door to a small closet. "This is the linen closet where we keep towels and bedding."

*****

The girls stepped to the bedroom. "This furniture is also a wedding gift from our folks."

Maria pointed to the window. "What's that?"

"It's an air conditioner unit," replied Angie. "I only run it to cool the room when it gets hot and humid. It's kinda noisy. Here, let me show you."

Angie turned on the unit. It came to life with a rattle then settled into a loud hum. Maria stood fascinated in front of it as cool air washed over her. *¡Madre mía! She, her family, and neighbors had to congregate nightly on the roof grateful for any little breeze to provide respite from the hot, humid, stifling, stagnant summer air.*

"It's not so bad tonight," said Angie turning of the unit.

Maria turned to look at Angie and Bill's framed wedding portrait on the dresser. "You're a really good looking couple."

"Thanks."

*****

They checked out the bathroom. "The blue toothbrush

is mine. The red one is Bill's." Angie wiped her eyes
with her fingers. "Jeez! Here I go again." Angie paused
for a moment, sighed, and placed her hand on Maria's
shoulder. "Okay. You go unpack your things and I'll
make us some supper. Okay?"

Maria nodded and carried her suitcases off to the living
room.

*****

The girls ate chicken stew at the kitchen table. Bread
and two glasses of water were on the table. Popular
music played from the kitchen radio – sometimes news
about the war.

"Mmmm mmmm! Delicious," exclaimed Maria.

"Mom's recipe. Chicken stew is a favorite at our house.
Where'd you and Mateo live?"

"Never did. Just got hitched last week. Thought I told
ya that."

"Yeah, you did. Just forgot. So how did you get your
private moments?"

"Sometimes on the roof, sometimes the alley. Always
at night, y'know. We would smooch and touch a lot. We
fooled around whenever we got a chance. Sneaky and so
much fun." Maria placed her elbows on the table, rested
her chin on her interlocked fingers, and grinned with
a wistful look. "Yeah. Felt so good when we did that.
Y'know what I mean by foolin' around, right?"

"Of course. Did you use protection?"

"Yeah, did the consummation thing last week. First and
only time for me like that." Maria chuckled. "Saved
myself for marriage like a good Catholic girl. He threw
me a quick hump. Was great for him. Me not so much…
That was my freakin' honeymoon! On the freakin' roof!"

"At least you love each other, right?"

Maria shrugged. "Who knows?"

"Did he have a job?"

"Oh sure. He graduated Gompers vocational. Learned
about building construction. He was an apprentice at
a union shop in Manhattan. Not much pay to start, but
enough to get by to help out with his family."

"Sounds responsible."

"He is. He is. Then last month the draft called him up. Y'know the rest of the story. Like I said, he wanted me to get benefits in case somethin' terrible happens to him. So we got a quickie marriage in the courthouse…I'm so scared to even think the words *survivor benefits*."

"Those two words scare the hell out of me too." The radio was playing Sophie Tucker singing *After You've Gone*. Angie's eyes misted over.

"You okay?" asked Maria.

"Yeah, yeah. I hate those lyrics. They remind me how much I miss Bill. I'm so scared he might not come back." The girls held hands and pressed their heads together. They leaned back in their chairs and sat quietly for a few moments. Then once again they locked gazes, mesmerized! *What's going on here?*

Now *Stardust* played from radio. Angie had a sudden panicked look and buried her face in her hands.

"You okay?" asked Maria.

"Yeah, yeah. It's our favorite song." They gazed contemplatively at each other for a few moments. Angie rose from her seat. "I like to go to bed early so I can get up early to get ready for work. I have to catch the bus by seven. You mind doing the dishes?"

Maria gasped at Angie's request. She gripped Angie's upper arms and gazed straight into her eyes – her startled eyes. "What? What? Did I insult you? I apologize. I didn't mean to say that like you're my maid."

"Do I *mind*? *Really*? Are you kidding? You actually asked me if I *mind*? ¡*Madre mía*! How can you ask me that? Ya treat me like an equal. Don't talk down to me like I'm a freakin' dumb *chica*! On toppa that ya gimmee a way outa South Bronx hell and, and, and ya share your beautiful home with me. And…"

Maria released her grip from Angie's arms and held up her right hand. Her thumb and index finger almost touched. "Got any idea what it means for someone like me t'get even *this* much respect from a white person?"

Angie stared at Maria's hand in stunned silence.

"Uh huh! Uh huh! Didn't think so." Maria flung her arms wide open. Angie recoiled from her explosive gesture.

"*This* much! *This* much respect is what you're givin' me! I hit the freakin' jackpot! *¡Madre mía!* This is better than winnin' the Irish Sweeps."

Maria pressed her palms to her own temples. Tears poured down her face. "And, and all ya ask from me for this is give you some company? You don' even care if I chip in for rent or groceries? Company? *Just company? ¡Madre mía! ¡Madre mía! ¡Madre mía!*"

Maria again gripped Angie's upper arms and gazed into her eyes. "Here, here I'm touchin' you and lookin' at you and still can't believe you're real, that you're really happening to me."

Maria calmed down, kept her grip and gaze on Angie. "So how can you possibly ask if I mind doin' the dishes? *The dishes? ¡Madre mía!* I know you for only a day and would go to the ends of the world for you. So, no, I don't mind doin' the dishes. Now go! Go do whatever you gotta do for bed."

Maria's tirade stunned Angie. "I, I, I don't know what to say."

"Your respect. Your respect says it all!" Maria released her grip on Angie. "I'm sorry, Angie. Please forgive me. I didn't mean t'raise my voice at you, *especially* at you. I'm not used to bein' treated so nice outsida my family, especially by most white people."

Angie held Maria's hands and looked directly into her eyes. "Maria, I hope, I really hope you will think of me as family. And, and one more thing. Don't ever say that S-word again."

Maria agreed with a smile and a nod. Angie exited the kitchen.

*****

Maria washed the dishes and hummed one of her favorite songs, *Besame Mucho.*

She mentally reviewed the day before, the wonderful serendipitous day Angie and Bill fell – actually bumped – into her life. Everything, yes, everything that Angie did was beautiful in Maria's mind. Even the mundane sounds of Angie brushing her teeth, peeing, flushing the toilet, washing her hands. ¡Besame mucho! Yes, Maria did want to kiss Angie a lot for giving her life a new start. A feeling of tingly joyful chills washed over her.

She finished the dishes, wiped her hands, and stepped to the living room.

*****

Maria stared at the sofa-bed. She removed the two cushions, but was puzzled as how to open it.

The only bed she's known most of her life was the bunk bed she shared with her little brother, Angelo. She took the top bunk because she was taller, couldn't sit up without bumping her head in the lower bunk. Wait a minute! Angelo? Angelina? !Madre mía! Why hadn't she realized until this very moment that angels were always meant to be in her life? Maria's hands cupped her face, a face surprised by her eureka moment.

Maria snapped out of her trance. Yeah, the sofa-bed! *How the hell do you open this thing?* Maria didn't want to disturb her angel who was probably asleep. On the other hand, it was either that or else sleep on the sofa. Maybe Angie was still awake. Maria walked over to the bedroom. Its door was open. Angie lay partially covered by a sheet. Asleep? Maybe not. Maria lightly tapped the door jamb and whispered. "Angie?"

Angie opened her eyes and looked at Maria standing in the doorway. "What's up?"

"I can't figure how to open the fold-out."

"What's the matter with me? I just assumed you knew how. I'm so sorry. Let me show you."

Angie pulled aside the sheet. She wore only a nightgown long enough to reach her knees. Her legs swung out from under the sheet. The nightgown rode up and exposed Angie's naked lower torso. Maria was taken aback. Angie stood and readjusted the nightgown to cover herself. "What's wrong?"

Maria was flustered. "Oh, uh, nothing!"

"Okay then," said Angie puzzled by Maria's behavior.

They returned to the living room.

*****

"You removed the cushions. Good. Now grab the bottom there with your palms up." Maria did that. "Now lift up and toward yourself." Maria followed Angie's directions. The folded mattress was now exposed. Angie continued. "Good. Now grab the front of the mattress frame and bring it forward." Maria did that. The mattress opened flat and the whole assembly rested on the floor.

Angie smiled. "See? Duck soup. Now let's get some bedding."

She noticed Maria's small suitcase on the floor. "You didn't unpack that?"

"Just keepin' my underwear and socks there."

Angie looked at Maria, touched her shoulder, and smiled. "You're home now, girl. No need to live out of a suitcase. There's an empty drawer, lower right, in my dresser. Go use it. I'll get the bedding."

Maria still couldn't believe how she lucked out having this person come into her life. Now she offered to share a little part of her bedroom. ¡Madre mía! How much more personal can you get than your bedroom? Yeah, okay, the bathroom.

*****

The girls spread the sheets and blanket. Angie tossed a pillow onto the fold-out bed. "There you go. Ready for beddy-bye."

Angie seated herself on the sofa. Her expression took on a serious demeanor. She pointed toward the open fold-out. "Please sit there and look at me." Angie's strict look startled Maria, like a nun about to rap her knuckles. Maria nervously seated herself on the fold-out mattress.

"You looked uncomfortable when I got off my bed. Why?"

Maria was flustered. "I dunno. Did I?"

"Did my nakedness bother you? I'm a girl, you're a girl. Didn't you ever see girls naked?"

Maria became more upset. "Only in high school gym class. And we rushed to cover up. Never stared at one another. Afraid we'd be called a *maricóna* if we did."

"What's that?"

"That's a Spanish insult for a lesbian. Y'gotta understand. I never saw nobody all naked at home. Not my folks or even my little brother since he was a baby. Now *this* is my home and I was shocked to see ya that way even if it was just for a little bit."

"What about you and Mateo?"

"We were never naked together. Only fooled around outside with our clothes on. Always rushed, scared t'get caught."

Strange! Nothing frightened Maria on the South Bronx mean streets. However, the shame, the thought of being completely naked among others frightened her. The curse of a strict religious upbringing most likely beat that fear into her.

Maria trembled looking nervous and frightened. She looked away from Angie, then looked back at her, still trembling. "Please, Angie, can we please stop talkin' about this?"

Angie sat quietly for a moment staring at Maria. She rose from her seat. Maria was mesmerized by Angie's beauty. *¡Madre mía! That unbelievable beauty! Her raven hair, dark eyes, alabaster skin, nipples poking against her flimsy white nightgown. Like an unreal apparition!*

Maria opened her mouth to speak. Angie pressed her finger against Maria's lips before she could utter a sound. "Shhhhh!"

Angie moved closer and gripped Maria's wrists. Maria flinched. Angie tightened her grip. She stepped back pulling Maria to a standing position. The girls gazed at each other. Maria remained mesmerized. Angie caressed Maria's face. She turned her head aside with a look of trepidation. "Please, Maria. Please look at me." She looked back at Angie.

"I need you to understand something," said Angie.

"O…kay."

"While our guys are away this is now *our* home. Got it? *Our* home. We're going to live together for a while.

Right?"

"Uh huh."

"That means we have to trust and be comfortable about everything. No secrets. Think you can do that?"

"Uh huh."

"So you might see me naked when I get out of the shower. Think you can handle that?"

"Yeah, I think so."

"So it's up to you if you wanna let me see *you* naked. I don't care one way or another. Okay?"

Maria felt relieved. "Yeah, thanks."

Angie impulsively hugged Maria and gave her a quick peck on her cheek. Maria was surprised and shocked as their bodies pressed together. Their bodies parted. Angie rested her hands on Maria's shoulders and looked at her. "Good! That makes me happy. Now let's get some sleep. I have to get up early. You just sleep in and later explore the neighborhood. I'll leave your apartment key on the kitchen table. Night. Sleep tight."

Angie gently stroked the side of Maria's neck with her finger. A slight shiver shot through Maria's body. She touched that spot and shook her head with a look of wonder and admiration as she watched Angie leave the living room. Angie turned to look back at Maria – winked. She sent Maria a Mona Lisa smile just like they sent each other at Penn Station.

Back at her bedroom, Angie retrieved a V-Mail envelope from a side table drawer. She wrote Bill a letter.

My dearest darling Bill,

That Spanish girl moved in with me the day after you left. Her name is Maria Torres. She's 19. So don't worry about me living alone. I think we'll be good friends. She likes to swing dance too. My heart aches so much because I miss you so much. I can't wait for you to come back so we can make our baby.

With all my love, Angie

*****

Angie approached her apartment after returning from work the next day. A light delicious aroma permeated the hallway. She unlocked and opened the apartment door. The aroma blasted her nose at full strength. "Jeez! What *is* that delicious smell?"

"*Frijoles y arroz*. Whoops! I mean beans and rice. See? *¡No mentí!* I told you I was a good cook."

Maria placed two plates of food and two glasses of water on the kitchen table. Angie seated herself at the kitchen table and took a forkful.

"Jeez! This is so delicious."

"I made it with *Mamá*'s special sauce. Used just a little pepper this time. Hope it's not too hot. Water there just in case."

"No! No! It's perfect. I never ate anything so delicious."

"It's simple and nutritious. Big deal with Latinos, y'know. Chew nice 'n' slow so ya can savor the flavor."

*****

Despite having impeccable manners, Angie literally licked her plate clean. Maria chuckled at that. "What's so funny?" asked Angie.

"I guess you liked it."

"Liked it? I loved it! I hope you made more. I'd love a little more."

"Sure did." Maria got the pot from the stove and ladled more beans and rice onto Angie's plate.

Angie again gobbled her food.

"Hey! Slow down. Savor the flavor."

Maria rested her chin on her hands and watched Angie eat. She was overwhelmed with joy that this simple meal gave her so much pleasure. It was such small payment for all that she was receiving from her new friend – her new wonderful *amiga*.

"Where did you get the stuff to make this?"

"I took your advice and explored the neighborhood. I looked inside several stores. One of them was Berski's Grocery."

"Oooo! Oooo! That's where I get my, uh, where we'll get our groceries. What do you think about Mr. Berski?"

"What a nice man! So friendly. I was new to him, so I told him about me and Matco. He said he has a young customer whose husband also joined on Sunday. So I asked him for her name. He was surprised when I told him I was livin' with you and how we met. Boy, that man loves t'talk about you. Thought I would never get outa his store."

"Yeah. He's a chatty one."

"He seems a little sad."

"Yeah. His wife is really sick, doesn't expect her to last much longer."

The girls continued to eat. Occasional tender gazes lingered between them.

"Oh, this is *sooo* good!" Angie wiped her mouth with a napkin. Stood, went to the stove, and looked into the pot. "Oh, good. There's lots more."

Maria started to rise from her seat. "I can get it."

Angie held open her palm toward Maria. "Sit. Sit. I just want only a little bit more." Angie got her plate, ladled a small amount of beans and rice onto it, and returned to her seat.

They continued to eat. After a long silence, Angie said, "I may have some good news for you."

They continued to eat. Another long silence.

"Y'gonna tell me? Or what?"

Angie, impish smile, took another bite. Again a long silence.

"Stop futzing around. Tell me!"

"I went to personnel and told 'em you're a bookkeeper and a Navy wife with no kids."

"So? So? Were they interested?" Angie took another bite. Again a long silence. Exasperated, Maria glared at her.

"Easy, easy! Take it easy! Your bookkeeping experience sounds perfect for inventory control for the F6F Hellcats they're building there. That's a new carrier fighter. They need to hire more inventory staff."

"Did they say I could come in for an interview?" Angie took another bite. Again a long silence. Maria glared and shook her fists. Angie chuckled and raised her hands in feigned fright. "Ooo! So scared! You sounded like a shoo-in for the job. I told 'em I'll bring you by tomorrow."

The next day, Maria waited for Angie at the bus stop outside the Grumman plant. She jumped up and down when she spotted her leaving the building. Maria ran to Angie and lifted her off her feet with a tight hug. Angie broke into laughter. "Wait! Wait! Don't tell me. Ummm, you got the job?"

"I got it! I got it! I got it! I start tomorrow morning for training. I can ride with you. I can't believe this is all happenin' so fast just because you came inta my life. Thank you, thank you, thank you. I can now pay my folks back a lot sooner. Even send 'em some regular extra. And buy a coupla pretty dresses like you got. Isn't that great?"

"Yes, it *is* great!"

*****

The girls bus-rode home. Maria rested her head on Angie's shoulder and hugged her arm. They didn't talk much. There was no need to. Angie's loving glances at Maria and Maria's exuberance did all the talking for them.

They got off at their stop. Maria had an idea. "Hey! Let's celebrate my new job. I wanna get some groceries to make a special dish for my special roomie." They walked over to Berski's Grocery. It was closed. The girls read the scribbled note taped to the door.

Closed. Open soon as possible. I.B.

"Oh, no," cried Angie.

"What?"

"Mrs. Berski. I think it's Mrs. Berski."

The girls rushed to their apartment building. A crowd of grieving neighbors gathered in front of the building. Angie approached one of them. "Mrs. Goldfarb, what happened?"

"Sofia, Sofia pass away last night. Yitzhak is at funeral home," she said with an east European accent.

Angie's eyes moistened. "We were expecting this for a long time. It still hurts when it actually does happen."

Mrs. Goldfarb glanced at Maria with a sneer. She looked back at Angie. "A Puerto Rican?"

Maria stared at Mrs. Goldfarb. "Hey! *Señora* Goldfarb." She looked back at a frightfully glowering Maria. *"¡Eres una vieja loca!"* Mrs. Goldfarb didn't understand a word of Spanish, but Maria's tone and glower sent terrifying chills through her frumpy body. The girls doubled over with laughter. They turned to enter their building.

"Funny?" Mrs. Goldfarb shouted. "You think that funny? That not funny!"

Angie's laughter instantly turned to anger. She grabbed Maria's arm and dragged her back toward Mrs. Goldfarb. "Know what's not funny, Mrs. Goldfarb? You're not funny. Maria's Puerto Rican husband is out in the Pacific to fight Japs. Maria works at Grumman to build airplanes to fight Japs. What do *you* do all day, day after day? Kvetch, kvetch, kvetch all day long with other old yentas?"

Mrs. Goldfarb became angry. "Who you to talk to me like that?" She raised her hand as if to slap Angie. *Bad, bad, bad mistake!*

Maria gripped and twisted the old lady's wrist so as to whisper in her ear. "You do anything to hurt Angie I swear you're gonna get some serious *Puertorrequeña* hurt from *me*. Kapeesh?" Mrs. Goldfarb was frozen with fear being held by Maria's painful grip. "I don't hear you." Silence. The other neighbors cautiously approached the drama. Angie, displaying her own rage, stepped in front of them with her opened palms to stop their approach.

Maria repeated her whisper. "I still don't hear you." Mrs. Goldfarb trembled with fear. "What you want me to do?" Maria's glower became a sadistic grin. "I want you to nod and say you understand. Now that's not hard to do for even a stupid old lady like you. Now *say* it!"

"I, I, I understand." Maria released her grip, turned to Angie, and laughed. "See roomie? The stupid old lady understands!" The girls laughed as they entered their apartment building.

*****

They sat at their kitchen table drinking tea. "That was so freaking funny," said Angie. "I thought she was gonna have a stroke. Be careful how you use that look."

"Oh, yeah? What about that look *you* gave the neighbors? I never thought a face like yours could ever look like that."

"Yeah, well. We're now social pariahs with the geezer crowd.

Maria gave her a puzzled look. "Pariahs? Is that some kinda fancy college word?"

"It means we're outcasts, personae non gratae."

Maria gave her another puzzled look.

Jeez! I sound like a freaking pretentious snob. "Uh, it means they really won't like us," said Angie.

"I ain't gonna lose sleep over that," replied Maria. "You?"

Angie smiled and shook her head. "Are you ever gonna tell me what you said to her?"

"Not important. Trust me, she ain't gonna raise her hand to you again."

"Yeah, well, that and your look must have scared the crap out of her. You are one tough chick."

"Gotta protect the ones I love."

"You love me?"

Maria gazed at Angie. Pondered. "Let's see...On Sunday you made me your friend. Yesterday I moved inta your beautiful home from a rundown tenement. Today y'got me my first full-time job...So? Do I love you? Hmmmm!...Lady, I freakin' *worship* you! In only three freakin' days!" Maria snapped her fingers. "Three! Just like that y'turned my life around in so many wonderful ways. How else can I *possibly* feel?" Maria's effusive display of affection stunned Angie.

"What? Can't say how I feel? Remember our deal? No secrets." Angie nodded and gazed trance-like at Maria. Maria returned her own gaze.

Angie snapped out of her trance. Her thoughts returned to Mr. Berski's loss. She slumped back into her chair looking very sad. "Wonder how Mr. Berski's dealing with this," said Angie. "Poor guy. He loved her as much as life itself...Actually, Mrs. Berski *was* his life. My heart breaks for him." Angie sighed and stared deadpanned into space. "I don't feel like eating. Maybe just some toast and a glass of milk." Maria touched Angie's shoulder as Angie started to rise from her chair. "Here. Lemme do that." Maria toasted a slice of bread, poured a glass of milk, and served the food to Angie. She lovingly watched her eat.

Angie finished her snack and went to her bedroom.

*****

Street lights through the curtains bathed the bedroom in a dim light. Angie stood at the dresser, raised her and Bill's framed wedding portrait, and kissed his image. Her eyes turned misty. She set the portrait down and changed into pajamas this time instead of that nightgown. She covered herself with a sheet, hugged, and kissed Bill's pillow. The pillowcase had become lipstick stained from Angie's kisses. She inhaled his fading scent and murmured. "Oh Bill." She snuggled his pillow and drifted off to fitful sleep.

*****

Angie lay in bed with a drowsy blissful smile on her face. Maria, also in pajamas, tapped the door jamb and whispered, "Angie?"

Startled, Angie replied. "Oh, huh, what? What's up?" Maria was so nervous about disturbing her angel. "Can... can I lay next to you?"

"Uh, oh sure, sure." Maria noticed that Angie hugged Bill's pillow. "Oh, uh, I'll be right back." Maria hastened out of the bedroom and returned with her own pillow. She hesitated to move toward the bed.

Angie scooched to Bill's side, turned aside the sheet, and exposed a mattress space. She patted the mattress beckoning Maria to lie next to her. "I won't bite!"

Maria slid under the sheet and lay on her back. Angie turned on her side with her back to Maria and snuggled Bill's pillow. They drifted off to sleep.

Next morning the girls ate a breakfast of scrambled eggs, toast, and coffee. "That was nice what you did for me. You know, keeping me company. I dreamed about Bill snuggling me. I miss that so much," said Angie.

Maria looked confused. She glanced at Angie, at her food, back to Angie.

"What's wrong?" asked Angie.

"I'm kinda mixed-up about something. I really, *really* need to talk about it when we get home after work. Okay?"

"Sure, sure thing. Of course."

Mr. Berski

Later that day after work the girls stopped off at Berski's Grocery. The small bell's tinkle announced their presence. The store was a typical post-Depression small neighborhood grocery store. Canned goods and packaged staples lined shelves on two sides. A small island in the entrance aisle contained several bins for vegetable and fruit items. The refrigerated case for perishables was behind the small counter at the end of the aisle.

Mr. Berski, in his 60s, rose from his seat behind the counter. His aged face was friendly and lovable. His body was a bit paunchy, about 5'8", spoke with a slight east European accent, slightly broken English. He greeted the girls, however, not with his usual ebullience. "Hello Angie and…wait, wait…Oh yes, Marie. Right?"

Angie corrected him, "Maria."

"Maria, of course. I apologize. Angie, can you do for me a favor?"

"Yes, of course. What is it?"

"Can you come by my apartment this evening after I close up at eight o'clock?"

"Oh, uh, Maria wants to talk—"

Maria interrupted. "No! No! It can wait."

"You sure?"

Maria nodded. "I'll shop around for groceries while ya talk to him."

"Thanks, Maria. Yes, yes, Mr. Berski. I'd love to come by. About eight thirty okay?"

"That would be nice. Thank you."

*****

There was a small knock on Mr. Berski's apartment door. He greeted Angie with his typical warm smile. "Come in. Come in. So happy you here." Angie was pleased that his grief has dissipated a bit, outwardly at least. He directed her to the kitchen table. The apartment floor plan was identical to Angie's but with older furnishings.

"Sit, please sit." Mr. Berski seated himself across from her. A worn closed shoebox was on the kitchen table between them.

"You probably wonder why I ask you here." Angie nodded, her hands folded together on the table.

"Whenever you come to store I get such happy feeling. I tell you this because you look so much like my young Sofia, the love of my life." Angie's eyes moistened. She wiped them with her finger. Mr. Berski hastened from the kitchen and returned with a box of Kleenex. Angie dabbed her eyes.

He seated himself. "We meet many years ago in Lower East Side, about your age." His doorbell rang.

"Excuse me, Angie."

He answered the door, speaking to Mrs. Goldfarb standing outside in the hallway.

"What can I do for you, Sadie?"

"I bring a sponge cake for you."

Angie suppressed a chuckle as she overheard and recognized the voice.

"That nice. Thank you very much," replied Mr. Berski.

"Maybe I come in and visit a little bit?"

"Maybe some other time. I have company."

"Who?"

"A neighbor is who."

"What neighbor?"

"*Oy!* Enough already with the questions."

"Okay. Make a secret."

The overheard conversation amused Angie. She shook her head and suppressed another chuckle.

"Good night, Sadie. Thank you for cake." Mr. Berski shut his apartment door, returned to the kitchen, placed the wrapped cake on the counter, and seated himself at the kitchen table.

"That Sadie Goldfarb. "Yeah," laughed Angie. "I recognized her voice." Mr. Berski also laughed. "I know why you laugh. I hear what happened. I wish I was there to see. Maria really scare her, but she deserve it!" A fcw moments passed as their laughter subsided.

"She bring me cake. I am grocer and she bring me something to eat. What is that saying?"

"Carrying coals to Newcastle," replied Angie.

"Boy! I ask simple question and you pop up right away with answer. You must know lot of things."

"Maybe. But there's one thing I will never know."

"What?"

"I will never know how I got so lucky to know you."

Mr. Berski patted Angie's hand. "Oh, Angie, Angie, Angie! Okay, where was I?"

"Telling me how you met Mrs. Berski."

"Oh yes." He gazed at Angie imagining he saw his young wife that wonderful day. His eyes moistened. "Please give me a minute, Angie." A silent moment passed. He took a deep breath and dabbed his eyes with a tissue. He took another deep breath – another silent moment.

"We meet many years ago in Lower East Side, about your age. To make extra money I play violin in theaters. Many theaters in Lower East Side. Anyway, one evening in English class walks in this pretty girl. Her dark eyes like magnets to me. After class we talk. Her name Sofia Melnik. She also from Russia like me."

"So you spoke Russian?" asked Angie.

"Russian?" he scowled and feigned spitting into his hand. "Ptui! Ptui! Never! We curse Russian. We curse Russia. Matter of fact, our Russian not so good. We talk only Yiddish. It like a secret language. Russkies no understand Yiddish is why they make for us trouble. Well, one of the reasons."

"I don't mean to upset you," apologized Angie. "Why do you dislike Russia so much?"

"Dislike? Who says I dislike? I not dislike. I *hate*! You ask why? Cossacks massacre us in pogroms is why. We lucky to escape to America." He paused, reflected…

"Anyway, four months later me and my Sofia marry. She also sing with me in Second Avenue theaters to make extra money. We save money from different jobs. Eight years later we save enough to begin grocery business together."

"Any children?"

"My Sofia once pregnant but we lose baby. Terrible, terrible day." His eyes moistened. He dabbed them with a tissue and took a deep breath. "Sometimes we dance in living room with record player. That make her happy. My Sofia's beautiful dark eyes always make *me* happy. Then last winter my Sofia get very sick. My Sofia soon would die and my will to live would also die."

Angie dabbed her eyes. He grasped her arm. "You see, Angie, sometimes two people so much in love life not good without the other. I old enough to no more believe in miracles. But, you know what? A miracle happen anyway." He gripped Angie's hand with a sudden squeeze. The move startled her.

"Four months ago walks into my store this angel with perfect name. Same beautiful dark eyes like my Sofia." Angie grabbed a bunch of tissues and wiped her eyes.

Mr. Berski's eyes also moistened. "I again was living day life began with my Sofia. Day 42 years ago when my Sofia walks into English class." He slid his chair next to Angie, wrapped his arm around her shoulders, and planted a gentle kiss on her cheek.

"Thank you, Angie, to keep alive my will to live. You make like my young Sofia alive again." Angie and Mr. Berski were overwrought with tearful emotion. They eventually calmed down and wiped their eyes. Crumpled tissues piled up on the kitchen table.

"That is why I ask you here." He reached to open the worn shoe box. The doorbell rang again.

"*Oy!* Now what? Excuse me, Angie."

He looked at Ruth Pinsky, in her seventies, standing in the hallway. She spoke with an east European accent.

"What can I do for you, Ruth?"

"I see Sadie leave from your apartment."

"She bring me cake."

"What kind cake?"

"Sponge cake."

"*Feh*! This coffee cake better. Here."

Angie chuckled and shook her head as she overheard the conversation.

Ruth Pinsky's sensitive yenta antenna picked up on that. "I hear woman laugh. A young one. Already you have a woman? A hotsy-totsy? Sofia just pass away. Shame! Shame on you, Yitzhak." Angie stifled her laughter with not too much success.

"I know who?"

"You think maybe I keep list who you know?"

"Oh, mister mystery man! Shame, shame!"

"Thank you for cake. Good night, Ruth."

"I know who. It pretty one from 4B. Am I right? She married, Yitzhak. Shame. Shame. She live with nasty Puerto Rico girl. I know. Sadie tell me what happen. Shame! Shame!"

Angie doubled over with laughter, hard to catch her breath, snorted, gasped.

Hearing Angie's laughter, he struggled to suppress his own. "Good night, Ruth." He shut his apartment door and returned to the kitchen where Angie was convulsing with laughter. Mr. Berski joined her laughter as he placed the wrapped coffee cake on the counter to join company with the sponge cake. He once again seated himself at the kitchen table.

Angie wiped her laughter tears. "So, I'm a hotsy-totsy, huh?" They both again convulsed with laughter. "Shhh! Shhh! She first class yenta. Maybe listen at door."

"So what! Who cares?" said Angie gasping for breath. They eventually calmed down and wiped away their laughter tears.

"Tell me, Angie. Are old Italian women nosy like that?"

"Yeah, I'm afraid so," she chuckled.

They took a few deep breaths and calmed down.

"Okay, remind me again. Where was I?"

"I think you were gonna show me what's in the shoe box."

"Right. Right." He opened the worn shoe box full of old sepia photos, removed his favorite portrait of young Sofia, and slid it toward Angie. "Those eyes beautiful.

Yes?" Angie stared at the photo for a few seconds, stunned by her doppelgänger. She pressed her hand to her chest, gasped. "That's amazing. It's almost like looking in a mirror."

"See? Except maybe for clothes and hair style. That why I feel so happy when I see you. In my head I say *my Sofia*. You give me a gift. Thank you so much, Angie." He stood and touched Angie's shoulder. "I want to show something else."

*****

Meanwhile, back at apartment 4B, a cheerful Maria was preparing her Puerto Rican sofrito chicken. She hummed, sometimes sang some Spanish tunes as she flitted about the kitchen applying her culinary artistry. She lick tasted some sauce from a spoon and looked very pleased with herself. "*Mmmm mmmm!*" She glanced at the kitchen clock, wondering what was keeping Angie.

*****

"This my old violin. I save from theater days. My Sofia happy when I play this love song from old country, very famous." He played a wistful version of *Ochi Chernye*. Angie listened to his virtuosity with eyes wide astonishment. He finished the tune.

"That is so beautiful. What's it called?"

Ochi Chernye. It mean *Dark Eyes*. I play it because my Sofia's eyes so beautiful, just like you."

"Are there lyrics to the song?"

"Yes, in Russky. I not want to speak Russky."

"Is there an English translation then?" I would love to sing it while you play." Her request pleasantly surprised him. "Yes. Teacher write for me. Not exact, but good enough. I go get for you." He left the kitchen and returned with the English lyrics. He handed her the sheet of paper. "Please play it so I can get used to the tune." She studied the lyrics and hummed along as he played. "Okay, I got it. Would you like to sing with me?"

"No, no, no. I want to listen to you."

He played and she sang.

Oh your dark black eyes, full of passion eyes,

Oh your burning eyes, how they hypnotize!
How I love you so, how I fear them so,
Since I gazed at you not so long ago.

"Just like my Sofia! Like my beautiful Sofia!" He wept. "Thank you, Angie! My Angie! My Angie!"

"Did you just say *my* Angie?" Angie grabbed a tissue and wiped her eyes. "That's the most beautiful love song I heard in my whole life. And, and you called me *my* Angie. Not just Angie, but *my* Angie. Just like you always say *my* Sofia, never just Sofia."

Mr. Berski looked surprised, shrugged, held out his arms, violin in one hand, and bow in the other. "What hard to understand? Your beautiful dark eyes always remind me of my Sofia. So when you also sing in English, why not say *my* Angie?"

"Oh, Mr. Berski, you have no idea what that means to me. How do you say *my Sofia* in Russian?"

"We try to forget Russian because of misery they make us. I only say in Yiddish *mein Sofia*. Better yet is *mein shayneh Sofia* to say my beautiful Sofia." He buried his face in his hands, shook, and sobbed. Angie grabbed a tissue and wiped his eyes. "Oh, Angie, I miss her so much." They sat for a few quiet moments until he calmed down.

Angie touched his arm. "This song has a special meaning for me too. Bill once said the same thing. Not in the same words, of course. I asked him why he was afraid to come talk to me when we were in high school. Like this song, he also said it was my eyes." Mr. Berski smiled and touched Angie's hand. "You see? With great beauty comes great power over men. I keep you long enough. Maybe Maria worry."

"No, no, Mr. Berski. You have no idea what a great gift you're giving me. Please let me know if I can do anything for you."

He stared at her. "What?" she asked.

"My Sofia favorite name for me is *Yitzy*. Please look at me with your beautiful dark eyes and say again that name." Angie hesitated. She slid young Sofia's sepia portrait toward him. "It's not my place. You look at this and remember only her…remember only *your* Sofia saying your name." He gazed at the portrait and silently mouthed *mein Yitzy…mein Yitzy*.

 "Thank you. I think maybe Maria worry what happen to you." Angie stood to leave. Mr. Berski stood and kissed the back of her right hand. "Please, please take a cake for you and Maria."

The Mentor

Angie had a glazed look as she entered her apartment and placed the wrapped cake on the kitchen counter.

"You look weird," said Maria. "Gone so long. I got worried." She pointed to the cake. "What's that?"

"Cake. Coffee cake."

"Where'd y'get coffee cake?"

"From Mr. Berski."

"He asked you to come by to give you coffee cake?"

"No. That's not the reason."

"You were gone so long. How much time does it take to give someone a coffee cake?"

"Jeez! I said that wasn't the reason. You're not going to let go of this cake thing, are you?"

"Y'blame me? You visit him for something I thought was very important and you come back with just cake?"

"Will you just shut up and listen to me? I also came back with a beautiful love story. A couple of neighbors stopped by to give him cake while he was telling me his story. He offered me one of them. So enough already about cake, okay?"

"Okay, boss."

"I'm not your boss, you twit. I'm your friend. You're my friend."

Maria's eyes welled up.

"You sure get weepy for a tough streetwise chick."

"Well, your friend ain' on the street right now. Is she?"

Angie realized she crossed the line. "I am so sorry. I shouldn't have said that."

"Yeah, maybe not. Makin' me your friend is the best thing that ever happened to me…The best!"

Maria wiped her eyes with her fingers and opened the oven door. "Let's eat this before it dries out."

Angie's contrite demeanor changed to joy as she inhaled the aroma.

Maria removed a covered pan and scooped some food

onto two plates. She placed them on the table along with two glasses of water, eating utensils and paper napkins. Angie gobbled a bite.

"Slow down! Slow down! The flavor, the flavor! Savor the flavor!"

"You're amazing! A cook? You're a chef! A culinary goddess. I'm having a gustatorial orgasm! What is this?"

"Okay, college girl! Now you're showin' off. That's a made up word, right?"

Angie laughed. "It's a real word. Gustatory means taste. This stuff gives me a feeling like I just had great sex. Well, *almost* as good!"

Angie's effusive response to her cooking thrilled Maria. "Sofrito chicken. Sofrito sauce is basic for many *Puertorriqueño* dishes." Angie gobbled another bite. "Freakin' sake!" scolded Maria. "Slow down. Chew slow. The flavor, the flavor. Savor the flavor."

"Okay, okay. You're right."

Maria took a bite from her own plate. "Okay, now tell me about that wonderful love story."

Angie swallowed her food and wiped her mouth with a napkin. She related all the details about her visit.

*****

They had good laughs about the cake incidents regarding the two old neighbors.

"Wow! What a beautiful story! In love like that for 42 years," said Maria.

A serene, trance-like distant gaze lingered on Angie's face. "Yeah. They were perfect for each other. Started and ended every loving day together for 42 years. Bill and I were beginning to make a life together like that too."

Maria patted Angie's arm.

Angie's serene demeanor *erupted* into a screaming furious rage. "But noooo!!" she screamed pounding the kitchen table with her clenched fists. Maria recoiled.

"Those *fucking* Japs just hadda put a stop t'that! I hate 'em! I hate 'em! I hate those *fucking* Japs to hell!"

Angie's fist struck the edge of her plate, flipping it off

the table. Flying chunks of food splattered the table, the girls' clothing, and their faces. The plate shattered on the floor. Food chunks and ceramic shards made a mess. Angie took a few deep breaths, calmed down, buried her face in her hands, and whispered. "Please, Bill...Please come back."

Maria cleaned the table and floor messes with wet rags and a dustpan. She wiped their faces and clothing with napkins. Maria got a plate from the cupboard, scooped some sofrito chicken from the pan, served it to Angie, and planted a gentle kiss on her cheek. Angie responded with a sad smile. They silently ate. Wistful glances flitted between them.

*****

Having finished their meals, the girls gazed at each other for a few quiet moments. "Okay. What did you wanna talk to me about?" asked Angie.

"Wait," replied Maria, "let's do the dishes, clean up and get some fresh air."

*****

The girls walked to the park and seated themselves on a bench.

"Okay," said Angie. "Talk."

Maria scratched her head, but hesitated to start her explanation. "Okay, it's kinda like this, kinda personal."

"We're roomies, trust about *everything*. Remember our deal?"

"Yeah, yeah. Anyway, I went to bed last night a little after you did after we learned about poor Mrs. Berski. I was thinkin' about Mateo and how much I missed him. So I touched myself down there. As kids, the nuns told us it was a sin to do that. I felt guilty. So I stopped. But it felt so good."

"The nuns, yeah, the nuns! It never ceases to amaze me how convoluted medieval superstitions persist to this day of scientific knowledge. How they can promulgate—"

Maria stared at her with an upraised eyebrow.

"It's a word," said Angie. "It means to propagate, to disseminate, to make widely known, to—"

"*¡Basta! ¡Ya basta!*" interjected Maria.

Angie gave her a perplexed look. Maria smirked. "How ya like *that*, college girl? Throw fancy college words at me, I'm gonna throw back some *español*...I said enough, enough already!"

Angie laughed. "As I was saying, I'm amazed how they can destroy desire for sexual pleasure. It goes against all things naturally human!"

Angie shook a finger at her. "Now you listen to me and listen to me good. Get that religious nonsense out of your head. Don't let your life be ruled by a bunch of old men in Rome."

Maria was amazed how this woman could erase religious nonsense from her mind with a few logical comments. Maybe she should ask her views about Hell. Naaah! She already knew what her answer would be.

"If it makes you feel good and you're not hurting anyone else, then it's a sin *not* to do that. *Kahpeesh*?"

Maria nodded. "Yeah, I do. Anyway—"

"Another thing. Stop saying *down there*. The word is *pussy. Pussy, pussy, pussy*! Say *pussy*!" Maria hesitated. Angie gazed at her with that stern expression. "I don't *hear* you!" Maria took a deep breath and squeezed out the word. "*Puuuuusseeee!* There! Happy?" Angie smiled. "I'm not *unhappy*. Now go on with what you were telling me."

"Anyway, I then thought back about that quick hug and kiss ya gave me our first night. Remember?" Angie nodded.

Maria blissfully hugged herself. "Oh, it felt *sooo* nice. Not like *Mamá* or my aunts huggin' me. So I decided to take a chance to go to your room. Not for any hanky-panky. We're not those kinda girls. I just wanted ta feel good bein' next t'my, t'my…"

"Friend?"

"Yeah, my friend. I was so scared you'd be angry at me. But instead, you invited me t'share your bed."

"How *did* it feel?"

"Well, that's what I'm kinda mixed up about. During

the night I woke up when ya shifted around and your body pressed against me. It felt so nice, so soft, so warm through our pajamas. After a little while I felt funny, nice kinda funny like with Mateo. Is that wrong if it's with you, with a girl?"

"Funny you ask that. I awoke a few times myself when our bodies touched. I got a warm fuzzy feeling like that too. I didn't pull away. Didn't wanna pull away. I didn't wanna say anything because I know how you feel about, uh, about—"

"*¿Maricónas?*"

Angie nodded. They gazed at each other, pensive. "Okay, back to our talk," said Angie. "Remember how good it felt when you touched yourself?" Maria nodded. "Are the feelings the same or different when Mateo or you touch yourself like that?"

"I dunno. About the same, I guess. Feels nice."

"Just nice?"

"What's wrong with *nice*?"

"Nothing. It's just not nice *enough*. Let's go back and I'll show you what I mean."

*****

Angie stood next to Maria in the bedroom. She wrapped her left arm around her shoulders and whispered. "Now close your eyes, take a few deep breaths and imagine that Mateo holds you, kisses you, touches you." Angie planted a gentle kiss on Maria's cheek and slid her right hand into the front of Maria's slacks.

*****

They sat on the edge of the bed with Maria catching her breath. "*¡Madre mía!* I never felt anything like that my whole life. It was, it was—"

"Ecstatic? Euphoric? Rapturous? Sublime?"

"Yeah, yeah, one of your fancy college words! Maybe all of 'em! Whadaya call that feeling?"

"Orgasm."

"*¡Madre mía!* You used that word about my sofrito."

"Yup! It was *that* delicious! Now isn't that feeling better than just *nice*?"

"*¡Madre mía!* Are you kidding? Ever do that to anybody else?"

"No, just to myself. I can't help it now with Bill away."

"You do? When?"

"Sometimes when I hug Bill's pillow I daydream about him making love to me wrapped in his strong arms. Sometimes in the women's room at work." Maria looked shocked, stared open-mouthed at Angie.

"Yeah, that's right! At work…yeah, I daydream about him a lot."

*****

The girls rode home from work the next day. "How's the training coming along?" asked Angie.

"All done. Got assigned my warehouse section. I track every F6F part taken there and report to order more when the count drops to a certain level." They gazed out the bus window, lingering silence. Maria giggled. "I got a secret."

"Oh yeah? What?"

"Shhhh! Not here."

*****

The girls ate leftover beans and rice at the kitchen table. "Okay! What's your big secret?"

Maria giggled with an impish grin. "When I was alone by myself once in that big warehouse, I touched myself the way y'did t'me. *¡Madre mía!* It felt so good!"

Angie laughed. "Did you—"

"Oh no! Heard footsteps coupla aisles over. Mighta gotten caught if I didn't stop." Maria squirmed in her seat. "*¡Madre mía!* I gotta go take care of myself."

"Hold on! Let me show you something else Bill does to me."

*****

The girls stood next to the bed. Angie placed her hands on Maria's shoulders and gazed into her eyes. "Now I think you're really going to like what I wanna do."

"Better than last time?"

"Oh yeah! I know how you feel about being naked, but for this to work I have to see you a little naked."

"How little?"

"Waist down." Maria swallowed a nervous gulp. "Oh hell! I gotta stop bein' stupid about this. Besides, it's just you, not the whole world."

*****

They sat on the edge of the bed gazing at each other. Maria was naked below her waist. Angie grinned. "*Sooooo*? Howjah like it?"

"Are you kidding? That…was…ah…may…zing! I orgasmed…Is that a word?" Angie nodded. "I think I orgasmed three times!"

Angie grinned. "It *was* three. I know. I was there."

Maria stared eyes widened. "That *was* better than last time! I never knew people did that." Maria was a bit nervous as she moved her face closer to Angie's. Their fingers interlocked and their lips almost touched. Maria hesitated. Then she planted a gentle, wondrous, unhurried kiss on Angie's lips.

"I really wanted to do that."

"That was nice! I'm glad you did," said Angie.

Maria took a deep breath. She pondered Angie's smiling dark eyes.

Maria sat deep in thought, overcome with guilt. How could she ever repay this angel for receiving so much? Escaped from South Bronx hell! Lived in a beautiful home, a home with an elevator yet! And an air conditioner! Cared about everything in her life! A remarkable life teacher, actually a mentor, and now being gifted with her first major orgasms, actually any kind of orgasm! She couldn't imagine such pleasure was even possible. And all she gave in return was some companionship and some cooked meals? Was she joking, just some cooked meals? No, enough was enough! ¡Madre mía! She loved Angie. Not just love like a dear friend, but in love like a lover. Her feelings about Mateo didn't even come close. How could she not be in love with Angie? She was drunk with love for Angie. Yes, in love with Angie. Can a woman really love a woman like she loved a man, both emotionally and physically? Is this what lesbian love

*was all about? She must, must return to Angie the same
pleasurable gift she herself just received. Must do it now,
right now!*

"Whatcha thinking about?" asked Angie.

"I'm actually buildin' up some courage t'do somethin' I
never done before. Somethin' I gotta do *now*! *Right now*!"

"Okay, what?"

"Gotta pay my fair share for livin' with you."

"Huh? You already chip in for rent, lights and groceries.
What else is there?"

"What else? What about those loving feelings ya give
me? I wanna make it a two-way street."

"What are you—" Maria pressed her finger against
Angie's lips. She stood and removed the rest of her
clothes. She stood completely naked without feeling the
slightest shame, which astonished Maria about herself.

Angie thumbed up her approval. "It *was* worth the wait!"

Maria smiled, then fixed a serious lingering gaze at
Angie. Angie picked up on that non-verbal cue. She
stood, stroked Maria's hair aside, and nuzzled her neck.

Maria closed her eyes, gasped, and shuddered. "Wow!
Okay! Okay! Now please do what I say and don't you say
a word. If y'do, my courage might crumble. So promise
me y'won't say a word. Promise?" Angie nodded and
pressed a finger against her closed lips. They exchanged
seductive, loving glances.

Maria slowly, seductively, lovingly undressed Angie
until she too was completely naked. Maria pressed her
smooth swarthy-complexioned body against Angie's
silky soft alabaster skin. *The contrast was a visual feast!*
Their lingering full-body caress filled them with chills
and thrills! Flesh tingled! *What erotic bliss!* They kissed
a kiss that intoxicated them with intense sexual euphoria.

Maria pointed to the bed. "Now lay down like I did
for you." Angie did that. Maria's kisses meandered down
Angie's body. Angie closed her eyes and smiled as she
imagined Bill doing that to her. She silently mouthed his
name, grabbed, hugged, and kissed his lipstick stained
pillow.

"You know what this makes us?" asked Angie.

"*Sí, dos maricónas,*" replied Maria.

"You don't mind?"

"Not if it's with you, love!"

Times Square

It was Saturday evening, August 15, 1942. The girls decided to go dancing. They were all gussied up. Maria felt so grand wearing one of her new pretty dresses. Angie helped her with the makeup. They sat together in the half-full Times Square subway car clutching their small handbags. Angie was so excited. "I can't wait to get to Times Square. The USO there is really nice and they always have great swing bands." Maria shared her excitement.

The girls sat quietly as the train rumbled on.

A shabbily dressed elderly man played a Spanish tune on his harmonica. One of his arms was wrapped around a pole for support. Maria beckoned him to approach. "*Señor, ¿sabe tocar Stardust?*"

He nodded. "*¡Claro!*" Angie caught the *Stardust* part and tossed Maria a surprised look.

Maria handed him a dollar bill and pointed to Angie. "*Por favor, lo toque para mi amiga mejor.*" He smiled and played a sweet, moving version. Angie's eyes misted over.

The door at one end of the subway car opened. Two tough-looking Puerto Rican kids, about sixteen, swaggered in. One of them pointed to the girls. "*¡Oooh, mira, mira!*" They shoved the elderly man out of the way. *Big, big mistake!* They stood hanging onto support straps in front of the girls. One of them stared at Angie who nervously averted her eyes. Maria patted Angie's knee. "I'll handle this, love," assured Maria. She then slipped her right hand into her handbag.

The second kid looked directly at Maria. "*¿Qué pasa mai?*" He grabbed his crotch and threw some air kisses at her.

Maria smiled sweetly, deceptively. She beckoned him to approach with her left hand. *Step into my parlor said the Spider to the Fly.* He leaned forward with a confident, cocky grin.

Maria whipped out and snapped open Mateo's switchblade knife. She pressed the blade tip against his crotch. Her smile instantly turned into her frightening glower. Her piercing eyes shot daggers into his. *"¡Vete de aquí cabron antes de que te corte su parajito!"*

Terrified, the kid jumped back. Maria laughed at him. *"¡Te cagaste del miedo!"*

He grabbed his buddy's arm. *"¡Salgamos de aquí. Es una bicha miedo!"* They ran out to the next subway car.

Passengers applauded, whistled, and sent Maria thumbs-up signs. She stood, smiled, and acknowledged their accolades. She bowed with her right hand waving the opened switchblade, then closed and replaced it in her handbag.

The girls seated the elderly man between them. Maria handed him another dollar bill. *"Por favor, una vez mas."* All in the car were silent as he played the tune. Some, including Angie, of course, were brought to tears. The girls kissed his grizzled cheeks after he finished the tune. The elderly man gave each girl an appreciative smile. He stood before them and motioned for them to move together. *"¡Juntas. Siempre!"*

Maria scooched next to Angie. "He said we should always be together."

Angie had a disturbing thought. *Always? How is that possible?* She let the thought pass. "Where'd you get that knife?"

Maria chuckled. "It was Mateo's farewell gift to his bride."

"What did you say to that kid?"

"Oh, that? I told the jerk to scram before I hurt him really bad. I laughed because he looked so scared. Then he called me a scary bitch." She again chuckled. "He's ain't wrong about that!"

"But, but, but you did it so calmly. And that scary look you gave him. Wow! Just like with Mrs. Goldfarb." Maria shrugged. "Yeah! It's my South Bronx look. Ya learn to act cool. Never show fear. It's a cultural thing."

"Why didn't you let me know about the switchblade?"

"Why? Be honest with me, Angie. If I told ya about it when I first moved in, wouldn't ya have wondered what ya got yourself into by inviting a tough street-savvy *chica* to live with you?"

"Promise to never give me that look again like at Penn Station. I don't need any nightmares."

"Ha! Not to worry. It's only for special occasions like this and any threats to my roomie. Like I said, it's a cultural thing."

"Now I really understand why your folks were thrilled for you to move in with me."

"Yeah, but we worry about my little brother. Hope he doesn't get mixed up with gangs."

"Anyway," said Angie, "I'm glad you're on my side."

"Always, love! *Always!*"

*****

The girls entered the large USO ballroom. Volunteers provided free non-alcoholic refreshments. Hundreds of military service men and civilian women danced and socialized. Several bands took turns to provide continual popular music. The girls mingled, danced, and chatted. They talked with soldiers and sailors at the refreshment table. Angie swing danced with a soldier. Maria slow danced with a soldier. Angie sat holding a tearful sailor's hand while sympathetically listening to him talk. Angie and Maria sat with several service members at a table. Sometimes the girls smiled, sometimes looked sad as they listened to their stories. Maria swing danced with a Marine. Angie slow danced with a tall sailor.

*****

The girls strolled Broadway a few hours later. All that swing dancing fun made them a couple of happy girls.

They read the New York Times building marquee.

SEABEES JOIN 1ST MARINE DIVISION ON GUADALCANAL AND TULAGI.

A foreboding dread crossed Angie's face. "What's wrong?" asked Maria.

"Just wondering if Bill is one of them. That's all."

They continued strolling among the street crowd. "Well, that was fun," said Angie. "Those young guys really miss holding a woman. Some even wept during slow dances because they so miss their wives and girlfriends. In fact, one sailor I sat and talked with just cried because he misses his wife and kid in Virginia so much. I held his hand and only listened. He just needed a woman's ear."

"Actually," said Angie, "there was one slow dance I did with a tall sailor. He was built something like Bill. They were playing *Stardust*. I closed my eyes and imagined I was dancing with Bill. I got a little turned on thinking about Bill." Angie's eyes moistened. "Jeez! I miss him so much!" Angie retrieved a handkerchief from her small handbag and wiped her eyes.

Maria took hold of Angie's hand. "I can't imagine how that feels," said Maria. "I got feelings for Mateo, but absolutely nothing like I think you do for Bill." The girls continued their stroll among the street crowd. "Yeah, but I can't get outa my head how worked up I got dancin' so close with some of those guys. Don't even know what it's like bein' held against a guy's body, especially in a bed. What do ya call it when ya like sex with men and women?"

"Bisexual," said Angie.

Maria thought about some of her dance partners. "Yeah, some held me real tight. Gotta admit bein' held by guys like that got me kinda worked up. How about you?"

Angie fidgeted with her wedding band. "Me? Oh, no! I can never imagine being with another man that way. Bill will always be my only one...*always*."

"Even if he don't make it back?"

Angie *gasped*. She glared at Maria with shocked, stupefied, horrified anger. "How? How? How could you...?"

Maria instantly realized she crossed the line by blurting out Angie's greatest repressed fear. *If only she could unsay her careless words. Her careless stupidity hurt her angel in the worst possible way.*

Maria clamped her mouth shut with one hand and

reached to touch Angie with the other.

Angie _smacked_ it away.

Her reaction shocked Maria. Angie trembled and cowered against a building wall – bawled. The street crowd parted to give them space. Maria cautiously approached Angie. Her hand trembled. She hesitated to touch Angie's shoulder. "I'm sorry! I made a mistake! I didn' mean t'say that! I wasn't thinking. I'm so sorry! Please forgive me. I don' wanna go on living if y'don't say you forgive me!"

Angie glanced at Maria's hand for a moment, then grasped it to her shoulder. Angie took several deep breaths, calmed down, and gazed into Maria's eyes. "I'm so sorry. I shouldn'ta hit you."

"No, no! I had it comin' for bein' so freakin' stupid." They embraced. Tears dripped down their faces.

"Let's never, never speak of this again," demanded Angie.

"I'm begging. I gotta hear you say it," pleaded a tearful Maria.

Angie's eyes and lips formed gentle smiles. She held Maria's shoulders at arm's length and gazed into her eyes. "I forgive you. How can I possibly _not_ forgive you?"

"I, I, I don't deserve you."

They took a moment to calm down and wipe each other's eyes.

*****

The girls continued their stroll along Broadway, then turned onto 42nd Street. They came upon a record store. "I heard about a new swing record at work," said Angie. "Let's see if they have it."

Angie talked to a salesman inside the store. "Do you have Jack Teagarden's _Dark Eyes_?"

He nodded. "Come this way."

The girls followed him to a record rack where he showed Angie the 78 record. "Please play it," she requested. He did so on the store's record player. Angie was thrilled and excited. "Two. I want two!"

She paid for the two records. The girls exited the store

with Angie hugging the record bag to her chest.

"That's a great swing tune," said Maria, "but why ya so excited about it?"

"Oh, Maria, it's special because it's a gift for Mr. Berski. It's a swing version of the beautiful Russian love song I told you about. One is for us, the other one for him. I can't wait to give it to him. Betcha he'll love it."

*****

The girls took an uneventful subway ride back home. *No tough kids to deal with this time. Angie didn't worry about that as long as Maria was there. Wow! She had her own bodyguard. That was funny! She looked so sweet and harmless sitting there in her pretty dress. It was hard to imagine looking at her that she was one tough chick.*

*****

The girls entered their apartment. Angie laid the bag with the 78s on the kitchen table. They really wanted to get out of their sweaty clothing.

They showered together – caressed and kissed as water cascaded over them.

Maria hugged Angie in their bed. *Yes, their bed! At least it was their bed until Bill returned.* Maria pressed her lips against Angie's cheek. Angie stared at the ceiling feeling Maria's touch but imagined it was Bill doing the touching. She closed her eyes and smiled. Warm rapturous delight flowed through her being.

A sudden terrifying thought struck her! Her eyes popped open! *Until Bill returned? Until Bill returned? What will happen to Maria when Bill returned?*

The Gift

The girls stopped at Berski's Grocery after work. The small doorbell tinkle announced their presence. Angie held open the store door for Joey carrying a large paper grocery bag. The girls glanced at him. Embarrassed, he rushed out the door.

"We really have to get him out of his shell. You get the things we need while I talk to him," said Angie pointing toward Mr. Berski.

"It is so good to see your wonderful smile again," said Angie as she approached the counter. Mr. Berski greeted her with a big smile. "Angie, you already know why it impossible for me to not feel happy when I see you."

"Yes. That makes me feel happy too. That's why we have a surprise for you."

"A surprise? What kind of surprise?"

Maria distracted Angie as she placed a few items on the counter. The girls shared impish smiles. Maria winked and gently stroke Angie's hand with her finger.

Their silent dynamic didn't escape Mr. Berski. *Something is definitely going on between these two.* Maria continued to shop. Angie turned her attention back to him. "Oh, uh, you'll have to wait for that. May we stop by your apartment tonight at eight thirty?"

"Absolutely! I wait for you."

*****

Mr. Berski greeted the girls at his door. Angie excitedly hugged the record bag to her chest. "Come in. Please come in. My goodness, Angie. You look so excited. What's going on?"

"That's because I wanna show the surprise we have for you. Could we use your record player?"

"Yes, of course."

Mr. Berski's old living-room furnishings showed various stages of wear. The record player he and Mrs. Berski listened to and danced to was on a small table.

"Do you like swing music?" asked Angie.
"You mean like Benny Goodman and Artie Shaw?"
"Yes."
"What's not to like? Why you ask?"
"You'll see."

Angie removed the record from its sleeve and placed it on the turntable. She switched on the record player and placed the tone arm on the starting groove. The song opened with a short trombone solo. Angie held her open palm toward Mr. Berski. "Wait! Wait!"

The *Dark Eyes* swing tune began. Mr. Berski gasped at the opening notes. Instant memories of his departed wife flooded his mind. His hands caressed his face – eyes widened with joyful wonderful surprise. He listened for about ten seconds. His joy turned to sobs. Angie moved to comfort him. His hands caressed Angie's face and looked into her dark eyes. He did not see Angie's face, instead he imagined seeing his young wife the day they met. "*Mein Sofia, mein Sofia, mein shayn, shayn Sofia,*" he sobbed.

Young Sofia's face faded back to the reality of Angie's face. He alternately kissed each of Angie's cheeks several times. "Thank you Angie! Thank you! Thank you! Thank you!" He and Angie embraced.

The 78 skipped in its final groove. Angie waved a finger toward the record player for Maria to stop that annoying sound.

"Do you have any Kleenex?"
"In bedroom on dresser," he sobbed. Maria hastened out of the room and returned with the Kleenex. Angie and Mr. Berski grabbed some tissues. Maria was caught up in the emotion and grabbed one for herself. They seated themselves on the sofa and gradually calmed down.

"Can you do for me a favor?" he asked Angie.
"Sure. What?"
"Can you play again and do with Maria a little dance?"
"Absolutely."

The girls moved the coffee table to make more dancing space. Maria cued the record near the end of the trombone solo. The girls held hands, bobbed their heads to the rhythm, and waited for the *Dark Eyes* tune to begin. They swing danced with care not to bump into living room furnishings.

Mr. Berski clapped his hands and tapped his foot to the music's rhythm. His smile returned. He noticed that the girls lingered for an extra beat or two or three whenever they got to a face-to-face position. Their feet kept moving to the rhythm, but their eyes seemed to smile endearing smiles. Mr. Berski sensed that these two girls share mutual feelings of love. It was none of his business, of course, so he kept his suspicions to himself.

"That was wonderful. Where can I buy such a record?"

"Mr. Berski, that's our gift to you," Angie answered.

"But why?"

"Why? You ask why? I'll tell you why. During my last visit here you gave me one of the most beautiful gifts I ever got. Your beautiful love story about you and Mrs. Berski. And that song, *oh*, that beautiful love song."

Angie took Maria's hand, looked at her, smiled, and looked back to Mr. Berski. "I told your story to Maria. It gave us a lot to think about our relationship together while our husbands are away. So, if you have time, can you advise us about that from your lifetime of experience and wisdom?"

"Angie, my dear, dear Angie. I *always* have time for you. I make tea. Let us talk in kitchen. It such comfortable to sit and talk. Yes?"

He followed the girls as they headed to his kitchen. He tapped his temple, smiled, pleased with himself that his perception about the girls' loving looks was spot on.

The Surrogates

The girls sat with Mr. Berski at his kitchen table, each with a cup of tea.

"Okay, ladies, what do you want to know from me?" Mr. Berski looked at Angie, then Maria, back again to Angie. He looked at them back and forth a few more times. The two women looked at each other. Neither knew how to start the conversation. He patiently waited with his palms up to suggest that one of them should say something. He finally broke the awkward silence.

"Okay, I begin. I see how you look at each other. I think you ashamed to say. Right?"

His getting right to the point caught the girls off guard. They sat looking at him with stunned expressions.

"Why such a look?" he asked. "You think maybe I not know what go on with women when men are away at war? Ladies, ladies, ladies. I not need to hear words. Your look says you two more than roommates. Much more!"

The girls looked at each other with mortified expressions.

"Aha! I thought so," exclaimed Mr. Berski.

"We are so embarrassed," cried Angie. "You must be so ashamed of us."

"Ashamed? Ashamed? You two become stupid all of a sudden? That most beautiful news! Tell me only how it make you feel about each other."

"Oh, Mr. Berski," exulted Maria. "The feelings are wonderful with Angie."

Angie was taken aback by Maria's sudden enthusiastic response.

"Even just thinking about her makes me glad to be alive," continued Maria. "Angie does for me loving things Bill does for her. So in my mind, she is sharing Bill's great love with me. Does that sound crazy?"

Maria's revelation stunned Angie. She grabbed Maria's arm with her two hands. "Oh my god, Maria! That never occurred to me. You are right. Because of our intimacy you are Bill's surrogate for me while he is away."

"Surrogate?" asked Mr. Berski. "That sound like fancy college word. What means surrogate?"

"Uhhh, that means a person who is a substitute for someone else. Maria is Bill's surrogate for me because I get feelings of love like I get with Bill."

"Wait a minute! Let me think," said Mr. Berski. "So, Angie, when I look in your beautiful dark eyes I see and feel same love like for my Sofia. Do that make you surrogate for my Sofia?"

Angie slumped back into her chair, caressing her own face with a look of wonder. "You are right! You are absolutely right, Mr. Berski! What an epiphany!"

"Epiphany? What with all the fancy college words with you?"

"She does that a lot," said Maria.

Angie laughed. "That's when you suddenly feel the important meaning of something. That I remind you of the love of your life."

Tears dripped down his face. "And such a wonderful gift that is for me! Thank you again my dear, dear Angie."

The three people held their hands together at the center of the kitchen table.

"So, ladies," said Mr. Berski, "it give me great pleasure to know you make each other happy during this terrible time. So enjoy what you have right now until war is over. Impossible to know about future. Only thing we know for sure is what we have right now. So enjoy life together. Yes?" The girls nodded to each other.

He looked at Angie. "This is amazing visit. Maria make you feel your love for Bill and she feel such love right back from you. Your beautiful dark eyes make me feel same love for my Sofia. Surrogate! Epiphany! Who knew from such things?"

Joyful tears moistened their faces.

Hello Joey!

Later that night, the girls sat staring at each other at their kitchen table.

"He's right," said Angie. "What we have right now is wonderful but my future with Bill is always on my mind...What about you and Mateo?"

"Yeah. What about me and Mateo?" reflected Maria. "Good question. I like Mateo. Just liking ain't loving. I don' even feel married. Not like you and Bill...why the hell did I let him talk me into it? Hardly know each other."

Angie didn't mean to ignore Maria, but at this moment she was lost in her own thoughts. She gazed trance-like into space. "Yeah...the best part is when we snuggle afterwards and talk about our future together with our baby. Sure, the sex is great, but it's the snuggling that turns it into a delicious loving glow. We hug, never wanting to let go of the feeling...Now I just snuggle his pillow and daydream about us being a family...I'm so scared he might never come back."

Maria was also lost in her own thoughts. "Don' even know what it's like to be in bed with a guy. Can't forget how worked up I got dancin' with those guys. Wish I knew how it feels."

Angie was still in her own thoughts. "Sometimes Bill would just grab me, hug me and I melt with that delicious feeling, that delicious ecstasy. You don't always need sex to feel that way when you're in love. A touch or a look or even a thought is enough...I wake up next to him and my day starts happy...He's my everything. I don't know what I'd do without him."

Angie's words sank into Maria. "¡Madre mía! I get that feeling when me and you snuggle. I bet the Berskis snuggled a lot for those 42 years."

Angie nodded, still in a trance. "We've been together for eight wonderful years. We didn't make love until we were in college. We were so nervous that first time.

That's why my feeling love for Bill is different than the way I love you."

Maria was taken aback, stared wide eyed at her. Angie, deadpanned, stared back. Both were silent for a moment. "You said it! You actually said those words for the first time."

They gazed at each other for a silent moment.

"How can I possibly *not* love you?" asked Angie. "You're my best friend. You give me so much loving comfort during this rough time in my life."

Maria kept staring wide eyed at Angie.

"How long are you going to sit there like that?" Maria kept staring her silent wide-eyed stare.

"Don't change the subject. Yeah, you might get an orgasm with some guy you just met and think you're in love. Then that wonderful ecstasy slowly wears off. You don't wan' it to go away. You wanna be held, to feel loved. Think he's going to stick around to snuggle? Most likely it's goodbye to Maria. You're left alone feeling used, feeling cheap, feeling unloved. Score! Pleasure one! Love zero! Is that the game you wanna play?"

Maria pondered, nodded. "But I'll never know what it's like unless I try, even if it ain't perfect."

"Okay. Tell you what," said Angie. "Let's take it one step at a time. See how it feels being alone with a guy you just met. See if you still get turned on like you did dancing at the USO."

"Got someone in mind?"

"Yeah, that shy kid with the burn scars."

"Joey?"

"Yeah, remember? We talked about getting him out of his shell and treating him to a soda."

"Uh huh. Yeah, sure. Why not?"

"Okay then. Let's get him that soda. He's really shy and sensitive about his wound, so see if you can get him to dance with you here in the living room. Sound good?"

Maria nodded.

*****

Angie rang the doorbell at Joey's apartment. A large

matronly woman wearing an apron opened the door. "Yes?" she asked with an Irish brogue.

"We heard what happened to Joey in the Merchant Marines," said Angie. "So we thought we'd like to visit with him. Is he home?"

"He's always home," came the reply with a frustrated tone. "What are your names?"

"I'm Angelina Ricci. This is Maria Torres. Our husbands are in the Navy."

The aproned woman cast a wary glance at Maria. Maria guardedly smirked at her.

"I'm Amelia Collins, Joey's mother."

A butch-looking chick, probably mid-twenties, approached the door.

"This is my daughter Jenny," said Amelia. "Jenny, this is Angelina and Maria. They're Navy wives. They came to visit Joey because they heard what happened."

Jenny scanned Angie head to foot and winked at her. Maria grasped Angie's hand. Her eyes shot daggers at Jenny. *In your dreams, bitch!* Jenny, realizing she crossed the line, was quick to catch Maria's silent message – brief awkward silence.

"Uh, how nice. I'll go get him." Jenny hastened away.

"Please come in," said Amelia. "Don't stand in the hallway."

Amelia and the girls stood in the foyer overhearing Jenny and Joey's indiscernible muffled voices. Jenny raised her angry voice a bit. "So that's it? You're gonna hide from women the rest of your life?"

Joey offered an indiscernible muffled response.

"Mama and I are sick and tired of you feelin' sorry for yourself. Sure, life ain't fair. At least you didn't come back in a damn body bag like some of your shipmates."

Joey offered another indiscernible muffled response.

"Listen! If you don't get off your fucking ass to meet them, I'm gonna drag you by your fucking hair."

Amelia was clearly embarrassed. "Oh my! No delicate flower, my Jenny."

Jenny dragged Joey to the foyer by his left wrist. He

turned the disfigured right side of his face away from
the girls.

"Joey, this is Angelina and..." Maria and Jenny stared at
each other for a brief awkward moment. "...and Maria."

"Hello Joey! We're *so* glad to meet you," said Maria.

Jenny kept her tight grip on Joey's wrist. "Say something.
Say something *now*!"

"H, h, hello."

"Angie and I love ice cream sodas. We'd love to treat
you to one at Ziegler's."

"I, I, I don't like to go out. I am ugly."

"Ugly? I don't see ugly. Do you see any ugly, Angie?"

"Absolutely not! We see a war hero. How can that
possibly be ugly? Heroism is beautiful."

"You shouldn't hide your wound," said Maria. "It's your
wartime badge of heroism. Show America that you did
your patriotic duty."

"Really?"

"Yeah sailor, really! Now show us that badge."

Joey hesitated. He slowly turned his head, showed a
little bashful smile. Amelia and Jenny looked at each
other and weeped.

"Thank you, Joey. Now how about letting a couple
of girls enjoy company with a war hero over some ice
cream sodas?"

"That sounds nice."

*****

Once inside Ziegler's candy store, they selected a
booth. The girls were sensitive to Joey's feelings about
his wound. Maria steered him to the bench so that the
right side of his face was toward the wall. "You sit over
there, Joey. I wanna sit next to you." Maria slid in next
to him. Angie seated herself on the opposite side. Maria
gently touched his left hand. "What's your favorite flavor,
Joey?"

"Vanilla."

"With chocolate syrup?"

"Y, yes, please."

"Angie and I love chocolate, all chocolate." Angie turned

toward the counter, held up three fingers, and called out her order. "Three ice cream sodas please, one white and black, two all black." Mr. Ziegler acknowledged her with a thumbs-up.

"We'd love to hear your war story, sailor," said Maria. "You mind tellin' us?"

"Oh, sure. I don't mind. I was a crew member on a freighter, the Pink Star, goin' to Britain last September. It was part of a large escorted convoy. My ship sank after bein' torpedoed by a U-Boat."

"Did ya all make it out before it sank?"

"No. Seventeen didn't. We had to swim through burning fuel oil. That's how I got my so-called *badge of honor*. A destroyer finally rescued us."

Mr. Ziegler served the sodas. Angie slid the white and black to Joey. "Mr. Ziegler, Joey is telling us his war story."

"I'm pleased to meet you, Joey."

"Th, thank you. Me too."

"So you're stayin' with your family?" asked Maria.

"Yeah, until I get a job. I like to work on cars. I think I can get a job fixing military vehicles at the Fort Hamilton Army Depot in Brooklyn."

"That sounds promising."

"Yeah. I couldn't get work as a Hollywood movie star because of my looks, except maybe in horror movies." The girls burst out laughing. Joey responded with his own laughter. The girls wiped away laughter tears with napkins. Maria put her arm around Joey's shoulders. "Oh! Oh! Oh, Joey! You are a funny, funny guy." The girls and Joey started laughing again. Their laughter tapered off. They wiped away more laughter tears.

Maria hugged his left arm. "Oh, Angie! You gotta feel that muscle. It's somethin'!" Angie reached across the table. "Wow! I bet you must have powerful body muscles."

He smiled a little bashful smile. "I'm pretty good there, I guess."

A slow Big Band song played from the store radio. "Oh,

I love songs like that," said Maria. "Do you like to dance, Joey?"

"I never danced much."

"Not even in high school?"

"No."

"Why not?"

"I was too shy to talk to girls."

"Really? You're doin' great with Angie and me."

"That's because you're both so nice and make me feel so comfortable."

"So you never had a girlfriend?"

"No."

"Joey, Angie and I have a record player and some dance records. I would very much like to dance with you. Would you like to dance with me?"

"That sounds nice. But only slow dances. I never tried to swing dance."

"That's not a problem. We have some slow ones."

Joey appeared happy. *What nineteen-year-old guy wouldn't with two attentive and attractive young girls?*

The banter went on for a while.

*****

It was time to put the plan into action, to leave Maria alone with Joey. Angie slurped to finish her soda.

"That sounds great you two. Look, I have some errands to run. Take your time and finish your sodas. Maria is an excellent teacher, Joey. I know you'll both have fun dancing."

Angie paid Mr. Ziegler for the ice cream sodas. "Be right back with your change, Angie."

Stardust played from the store radio. "Oh no!" she murmured experiencing a panic attack like never before in her life. She trembled with a look of profound terror, like seeing a ghost.

"Are you okay, Angie?" he asked handing her the change. "Huh? What?" Angie's shaking hand pocketed the change. She rushed out of the candy store, crying.

Grow up!!

Angie hastened down the street, still panicked, still crying, still trembling. She kept wiping her eyes with her tear-soaked handkerchief. She spotted Mr. Berski entering his grocery store. Angie looked both ways to avoid traffic and scurried across the street – grabbed his arm. "I gotta talk to you. Please, I gotta talk to you."

Her demeanor alarmed him. "Yes, yes, of course. Why?"

"I'll tell you inside. Please hurry." He unlocked and opened the door. They hurried in. He closed and locked the door. "We can sit and talk behind counter."

He got a stool from the storage area in back of the store. They each took a seat. He placed his arm around her shoulders. "Why are you shaking? I worry about you."

"I really, really need some advice."

"Before you say anything else, Angie, first take some slow deep breaths to calm down." He held her hands. She slowly inhaled and exhaled several times. She gradually did calm down.

"Thank you."

"Good. Now talk to me."

"I just heard a song on the radio that terrifies me I might be alone without Bill forever. I'm scared I won't ever have his baby, our baby. It's not fair!"

He retrieved a box of Kleenex from under the counter and placed it in front of her.

He was well aware of the strong love bond between Angie and Bill. It was the same kind of unbreakable love that he and his wife shared for forty-two years. But he had never seen Angie in such an extremely panicked state. She was pleading for his help. He needed time to formulate a response. Thinking…thinking…thinking. She had depended on him for advice in the past, but this time it was different. Very different! She had an urgent need. He was so fond of her, so he had better not make a mistake. What will be his approach? Thinking…

thinking…thinking. Aha! An idea!

"Fair? My baby Sarah die day she born. You think *that* fair?!"

Angie's eyes welled up.

"My beautiful Sofia get sick then death take away love of my life. You think *that* fair?!

Angie lost what's left of her composure – bawled. He dabbed her eyes

"I going to tell you story about fair. A fairy tale story."

"I'm an adult. I'm scared out of my mind and you're gonna tell me a fairy tale?"

"Yes. You *are* an adult but sometimes behave like little scared girl in fairy tale with nobody to save her from big bad monster. I tell fairy tale story because I love you like daughter. Like my baby Sarah never grow up."

Angie couldn't believe what she was hearing. She was pleading for serious advice from this man whose wisdom she worshiped. Has he lost his mind? Angie's profound respect for Mr. Berski kept her from screaming at him.

"A fairy tale? Are you joking? I'm hurting so much. Why are you hurting me more? Why are you being so cruel?"

"Sometimes it only way to teach important lesson to someone you love. Now listen to story. Yes?"

Angie nodded.

"Good. Long time ago was king and queen who have daughter, such a beautiful princess. Her kindness matched only by her great beauty. Her dark eyes have magic power. All the kingdom love her. Why? Because no matter how they feel, one look at her beautiful dark eyes make them feel happy."

Angie was quick to catch on that he may be talking about her. She pointed to herself with a questioning gesture.

Mr. Berski shrugged. "Who else? Anyway, one day visits kingdom a handsome prince. Princess' beauty and kindness make him fall in love. They get married. All kingdom is happy because they love beautiful princess so much."

Mr. Berski cast Angie a quizzical look.

"Yeah! Yeah! Bill and me."

"Good. Anyway, newlyweds rent little castle. Oh boy they happy. So crazy in love like you can't believe."

Angie's eyes welled up. Mr. Berski dabbed her eyes with tissues. He continued the story.

"A month later they hear distant bell. Oh boy, says prince, that is town crier. That guy never bring good news. So he sends messenger on horse to find out what's what. Prince, it is bad news, says messenger when he come back from town. A far away fire-breathing dragon approaches to make us all unhappy."

Mr. Berski cast a questioning glance at Angie.

"The Japs are attacking. I got it, I got it."

"Good," said Mr. Berski. He continued. "This *is* bad news, says prince. I must leave my beautiful princess to slay dragon. She will be unhappy and afraid without me. I don't want my beautiful princess to be unhappy and afraid. So he sends some emissaries to search kingdom to find for her a companion. Next day one of them brings pretty peasant girl, maybe a little younger than beautiful princess. Hey, pretty girl, asks prince, can you be full-time companion for my beloved beautiful princess until I return from slaying the dragon? Duck soup, prince! She is my beloved beautiful princess too, says pretty girl. Okay, says prince, you got the job with benefits. Now I must depart to slay dragon."

Angie choked back a tear. Mr. Berski again dabbed her eyes with a bunch of tissues.

"Yeah, I know. That's Maria," said Angie.

Mr. Berski waved his hands in the air. "Okay, Angie, that is end of fairy tale story."

Angie looked bewildered. "What do you mean that's the end of the story? Did the prince slay the dragon?"

"I don't know."

"Did the prince return?"

"I don't know."

"You can't leave me hanging like that. Not fair."

"Again not fair? Think! Not fairy tale. It really your story. No?"

"What are you talking about?"

"You figure out who prince, princess, dragon and companion. Who others?"

"Let's see. The king and queen are my folks."

"And little castle?"

"Our apartment 4B."

"What about princess' beautiful dark eyes to make all kingdom happy?"

"Sure, that's you. But why did you tell it like a fairy tale?"

"Why not? Story has dragon and I want to teach you lesson real life not like fairy tale, not always fair."

"Oh!"

He paused and gazed into Angie's eyes. "You born one of luckiest little girls in the world. Wonderful loving parents in nice home. Grow up smart. Marry smart handsome man, you love of his life like my Sofia for me. You have perfect life twenty-three years. Never alone. Always loved. Life like happy fairy tale. Now comes war. *Poof!!* No more a fairy tale for Angie. Life no more fair. Yes?"

He grasped her hand before she could respond. "Wait! That is, how you say, rhetorical question. Now you scared *might* be alone without Bill? *Might* not have baby with Bill? Please believe I love you when I say this."

He gripped Angie's shoulders, gazed into her eyes, and shouted. "*Grow up!!*" His uncharacteristic tone startled her.

He released his grip and softened his voice. "Stop being scared all the time. This real life. Sometimes bad things happen. More than two thousand Americans killed in Pearl Harbor. What about their families? No more *might* be left alone for them. Already left alone! Scared to be alone by death, not by a song. How many babies not born for them? You think *that* fair?"

Angie, sad, speechless, just stared at him.

"My dear, dear Angie. I could say I sorry to make you sad, but not this time. Be grateful you have perfect fairy tale life for twenty-three years. Some people never have minute like that. Some people only have misery and tragedy. Life never fair for them."

"No, no, you're right. I'm so ashamed, so selfish. I'm so spoiled by my good luck. I could only think about myself. Thank you, thank you, thank you for teaching me to think like a grown up, not like a scared little girl. I needed that tough lesson. I love you so much for doing that."

"Now you understand why I could not make happy end to fairy tale story. Yes?"

"Because we can't tell what's going to happen to any of us during a war."

"Exactly. Let us hope your handsome prince slays dragon, returns safe and sound and you have baby. Then fairy tale life can begin again. Maybe."

Angie kissed his cheek. They held hands.

*****

Angie sat on a park bench, pensively watching children in the playground. A small ball rolled toward her. She picked it up. A three-year-old little girl ran to fetch it. Angie's eyes welled up as she handed her the ball. Angie's two hands cupped the ball and the little girl's hands. "What is your name, sweetheart?"

"Katy. Why are you sad?"

"Because I wish I had a little girl like you."

"If ya did betcha she would be pretty like you. Please don't cry, lady. It makes me sad to see you cry."

"I don't mean to make you sad, Katy."

"I know."

Angie gazed yearningly at Katy. This sweet little girl represented everything she wanted with Bill. Her gentle grasp on the ball and Katy's little hands lingered for a moment – not wanting to let go. Angie released her grasp and watched Katy run back to the playground.

Second Fiddle

Maria sipped tea as she watched Angie enter and seat herself at the kitchen table. A box of Kleenex and some bunched up tissues were on the table. Maria's eyes looked like she was crying.

"Did ya see a movie?" asked Maria.

Angie shook her head. "I just strolled the neighborhood thinking. Sat a while in the park. Thinking about Bill, about you, about Mr. Berski, about the war."

"You look so sad."

"Yeah, well, we're living in sad times. Whadaya gonna do? You don't look so hot yourself."

Maria got a cup from the cupboard, poured tea from a kettle and gave the cup to Angie.

"Wanna hear how it went with Joey?" asked Maria.

Angie nodded.

"It didn't."

"Whadaya mean it didn't?"

"When we slow danced up close I could feel it was workin'. For Joey. For me? *¡Nada!* Absolutely nothing! I went to change the record and then..." Maria paused. Her eyes welled up as she gazed at Angie. "...and then I couldn't get ya outa my head. It suddenly hit me that I gotta be freakin' nuts. I couldn't go on. I made up an excuse to stop. Sorry t'get Joey all worked up like that."

Angie rested her hand on Maria's arm. Angie's gentle touch instantly overwhelmed Maria with a warm feeling. She, in turn, rested her own hand on Angie's hand. A tear dripped down Maria's cheek.

"I love you, Angie. I really, really love you for all your loving kindness and generosity. I don't need no guy. What I need is *you*! Sometimes in the middle of the night I get up and just gaze at you in the dim light while ya sleep. I always get this huge happy feeling. I still can't believe my good luck."

Angie gently stroked Maria's cheek with the back of

her fingers. Maria kissed those fingers. "Wanna know the real reason I'm cryin'?"

Angie nodded. Her eyes misted over.

"Because I'm scared, scared ta death because I know we can't be together forever. Bill will always be number one in your life. He's a great guy and the only guy you ever loved, ever wanna love. All we got is this…yeah…only this *temporary* loving friendship."

Angie's eyes welled up. They gazed at each other.

"Remember Eighth Avenue?"

Angie nodded. Maria pressed her clenched fists to her own chest. Tears dripped down her cheeks.

"I cried you were gonna go back t'Queens and leave me t'go back t'my South Bronx misery. Remember?"

Angie nodded.

"But y'didn't leave me. Y'gave me a way outa my miserable life. And when we hug, when we hug, when we hug, I never wanna let go."

They gazed at each other for a tearful quiet moment.

"I know my wonderful life with you can only last until the war is over, what with a life y'want with Bill and a baby. Y'didn't leave me back then, but eventually you will. That's how it's gotta be. Can't be no other way."

Inner turmoil overwhelmed and agitated Angie that she couldn't refute Maria's words. Actually, it was more than agitation, more like nausea. Angie pressed her hand to her stomach. Terrible thoughts, frightening thoughts flashed through her mind.

She was right! Maria was absolutely right! How could she ever believe she would fall in love, romantic love, life-sharing love with this wonderful girl? How could she explain this to Bill?

"You don' look so good."

"Kinda queasy. Not feeling good. I'm worried sick what you'll do after the war."

What will become of Maria after the war? Will she have to return to her miserable South Bronx existence? Maybe with Mateo, maybe not! Eke out a living to find part-time bookkeeping work? She felt so sick! Nauseated!

Helpless! Wished she knew a way to keep that from happening. There must be a way! Must be!

"Don't worry about that right now, love. Until then, let me just play second fiddle to Bill. That'll give me time to collect lots of great memories of you for after the war… whatever becomes of my life. Maybe y'can help me figure somethin' out later. I sure as hell ain't goin' back to no run-down tenement after livin' like this with you."

They sipped tea as they glanced at each other over their teacups.

*****

Maria slept. Angie tossed and turned next to her. She got up, took Bill's recently received V-mail letter from a side table drawer, their framed wedding portrait from the dresser, and went to the kitchen. Angie's sobs wakened Maria.

Angie sat at the kitchen table with a box of Kleenex, a glass of Alka-Seltzer, and several bunched up tissues. She held the V-mail letter in one hand and the framed wedding portrait in her other hand. She mentally visualized Bill kissing her lipstick print on the back of their small wedding photo at Penn Station as she read and silently mouthed his words.

My dearest Angie, love of my life. I miss you so much my heart aches...

Bill's vision faded as Maria entered the kitchen, touched Angie's shoulder, and gently kissed the top of her head. Maria sat beside her and wiped her tears.

"I can't sleep. I'm a freaking wreck thinking about Bill." Angie's frame of mind was further aggravated by her thoughts of Maria's long-term future – just wouldn't tell her about that.

Maria sat quietly for a few moments gazing at the love of her life. Yes, the love of *her* life. She rested her hand on Angie's arm, then got up. "Here, I'll make some warm milk to help you get some sleep."

"No, don't. My stomach doesn't feel right." Angie sipped some Alka-Seltzer. She pressed one hand into her stomach and grabbed Maria's arm with her other hand.

"I dunno what I would do without you."

*****

It was the next day at the Grumman F6F Hellcat main assembly area. Angie and her coworker, Maisie, were pushing a hand truck. Angie looked ill. "Maisie! I'm not feeling so good. Think I'm gonna pass out."

Angie's legs buckled. Maisie grabbed and steered her to a chair.

"Hey!" Maisie shouted. "Somebody call for medical assistance!" Another coworker hastened to an emergency telephone.

A medical staff nurse arrived a few minutes later. She crouched to talk to Angie, seated, hunched over, her arms pressed into her body.

"What's wrong, Angie?"

"I suddenly got this headache, back pain and feel queasy and a little dizzy."

"When was your last period?"

The question shocked Angie. "Uh, a little early this time. Just a few spots. You think? You sure?" The nurse was very sure. These were very common signs of early pregnancy. "Let's go see Doc to be sure."

*****

The girls bus-rode home after work. Angie was excited and overwhelmed with joy. "I'm having Bill's baby! I'm having his baby! Have to write Bill he's going to be a dad. I'm going to be a mom! We're going to have a baby! Wish he could be here to welcome his kid. Have to call my folks. I am so damn happy!"

On the other hand, it wasn't so joyful for Maria. On the day they met, she feared her angel would disappear from her life forever. Now she's going to care for Angie throughout her pregnancy and help her raise her child until Bill returned. Angie had no other choice but to disappear from her life. A disastrous double loss for Maria! She grieved the future death of her profound happiness with Angie.

Maria stared trance-like out the window. Her fingers wiped away tears. Random thoughts bounced through her troubled mind.

That's how it's gotta be. Can't be no other way. I'm really gonna lose the best thing to ever happen to me. Gonna lose her. So scared to be without her. How can I kid myself we'd be together forever? Because I'm still a freakin' dumb-ass kid. That's how. Gotta grow up, for godsake. Freakin' war ain't gonna last forever. Mr. Berski was right. He's always right. Hope we can stay together until then. Help her take care of the baby at least until Bill got back. I bet Angie can teach me to grow up. She's so freakin' smart. Not even sure how I'll feel about Mateo after the war. Not even sure I wanna be with a guy. Worry about that later. Yeah! Later!

"Why are you crying?"

Maria snapped out of her trance. "Huh? What? Oh, these are happy tears. I'm happy for you. Yeah, real happy."

*****

Angie was cheerfully writing Bill the good news in a V-mail letter at the kitchen table. Maria poured tea into cups at the kitchen counter.

The doorbell rang. Maria went to answer it. The Western Union telegram boy standing there with a yellow envelope in his hand alarmed her. "Mrs. William Ricci?" he asked.

"Angie!"

Trembling fear overwhelmed Angie as she approached and saw the yellow envelope.

"Mrs. William Ricci?"

Angie nodded as her eyes welled up. She stared at the envelope, her eyes wide open, paralyzed with fear. The telegram boy reached to hand her the envelope. Angie just stared at it. Maria snatched it from him. Angie's tremble became a violent tremor. She staggered to the kitchen table, sat. "Wounded, please, just wounded! Open it, open it." Maria removed the telegram and perused it. Tears instantly dripped down her face.

"What does it say? What does it say?"

"The Navy Department deeply regrets, regrets to inform, to inform you that your husband Lieutenant William

Ricci was, was killed—

"*Noooo!!*" wails Angie.

"…in action fifteen August 1942 during Guadalcanal Campaign." Angie, hysterically pounded the kitchen table with her clenched fists, crumpled the letter, and pressed it to her chest. She *gasped* for breath. "*Noooo! No! No!* That's when we went dancing! That's when we were having fun! *Noooo!*" Profuse tears dripped from her cheeks onto the kitchen table. Panicked! "Maria! Bill died while we were having fun! For godsake! While were having fun! While were having fun! Bill died while were having fun!"

Angie *gasped* for breath. "Maria, what am I gonna do without Bill? Forever alone without Bill. All alone with our baby. I hurt, I hurt so much. I'm so scared. What am I gonna do? I'm begging. Please! Tell me! What am I gonna do?

Alone? Alone? Damned if Maria would ever let Angie be alone. Sure, Angie would have loving and limited financial support from her parents, from her in-laws. But for how long? They were, after all, a generation older. What about day-after-day, night-after-night practical support? Who will pay all the bills when Angie could no longer work? Sure, there was the government widow benefit. But was that really enough to also raise a child? Angie didn't abandon her the day they met, so Maria be damned if she would abandon her angel at this critical time.

Will Angie marry again? Who knows? Angie's devotion to Bill and now carrying his child made that a doubtful scenario. The child will always keep Bill's memory alive. Maria met her in Penn Station the same day Angie conceived. Yes, Angie told her about that! These devoted friends held no secrets from each other. Being there at the same time and place emotionally connected Maria to that conception. She was suddenly thrust into the greatest roles of her life – street toughie to responsible adult – devoted lifetime companion – potential surrogate parent. Hmmm! Can a woman be a father figure?

Her street toughness was perfect preparation to assume a take-charge role to provide stable emotional support to Angie through this overwhelming disaster.

Maria rushed behind Angie and wrapped their arms together to embrace her. Cheek-to-cheek, Maria assertively whispered. "Listen t'me! I love you. I'm *always* gonna love you. As long as y'wanna have me here, you'll *never* be alone. We'll be a family. Both of us will raise your and Bill's baby together."

Epilogue

MARCH 1943

The labor was uncomplicated. It went fairly fast for a first-time mom – only three hours. Angie was now a happy mom to a healthy little girl. She sat upright in her hospital bed watching the four grandparents take turns to hold and kiss their newborn granddaughter. Maria looked uncomfortable standing off to the side. Disturbing thoughts raced through Angie's mind.

She was well aware that Maria felt awkward in the presence of the blood relatives. But Maria was always with Angie, day in and day out during the travails of her pregnancy, in sickness and in health. Yes, just like a married couple! It would now always be the same with the baby. Yes, the two women had become lovers, but they dared not openly admit that to anyone. The grandparents had their uneasy suspicions, of course, but they knew better to keep those thoughts to themselves unless they wanted to alienate Angie, to be kept from seeing their granddaughter. To the world, Maria was her friend and roommate. Nothing more, nothing less! To hell what anyone thought about their relationship! Considering Maria's background one may think she was the tough one. Maybe so! But that toughness paled compared to the ferocity with which Angie defended their friendship.

But wait! Angie was completely mistaken during this joyous moment. Angie's dad took Maria's arm and led her to the group. Angie's mom handed the infant to Maria. The new surrogate parent wept with joy as she cradled her *angelita* in her arms. The grandparents surrounded Maria and expressed their gratitude with hugs and kisses. Angie was relieved. *What the hell was I worried about?*

Just like Mr. Berski, Angie forever wore her wedding band, the unforgettable memory of a lost love.

ONE WEEK LATER

Angie and Maria sat with Mr. Berski between them on his sofa. He caressed and kissed the infant's head cradled in his hand. "What is her name?" he asked. The girls nervously looked at each other, which was understandable.

Angie selected a name that, in her mind, meant everlasting love. What could possibly be better than Mr. Berski's love for his Sofia? They had no idea how he would react – therefore, cause for their nervousness.

Angie placed her hands on her infant as a cautionary measure. Maria scooched to the edge of her seat prepared for whatever happened.

"Sofie," said Angie.

He *gasped*, couldn't catch his breath as if he were experiencing a seizure. Angie grabbed her infant. Maria hastened out of the room. Angie snuggled her infant with one arm and comforted Mr. Berski with her other arm. Maria returned with a glass of water and held it to his lips. He took a few sips and calmed down. He caressed Angie and little Sofie. Joyful tears flooded his eyes.

SIX WEEKS LATER

Angie snuggled Bill's lipstick-stained pillow as she napped. Little Sofie lay in her crib next to the bed. Maria stood in the doorway. Her face radiated boundless joy as she observed her family. Little Sofie's coo wakened Angie. Maria stepped to the crib where little Sofie greeted her with a happy coo and outstretched arms to be picked up. Maria carried her *angelita* to the bed and laid her on Bill's pillow. Angie snuggled her daughter and Bill's pillow. Maria planted gentle kisses on Angie's cheek and little Sofie's head.

Angie imagined it was Bill planting those kisses. Bill's pillow kept Angie's lingering sorrow from letting go of their last night together – as if she *never* wanted to let go. At that moment Angie felt bonded as a family with Bill and their baby.

1948

Angie recalled the day they met that Maria said she was *pretty good* in math. She had Maria browse through some of Bill's college math books to see if anything intellectually clicked with her. It did! Angie made an appointment for Maria to meet with a City College advisor. That in turn resulted in some exciting meetings with some math professors. And that was how Maria came to matriculate for the Fall 1942 semester at City College.

The girls worked out a plan to coordinate Maria's work and class schedules. Maria wasn't crazy about the required humanities courses with all the time necessary to read *sooo* many boring books. That stuff robbed too much time from her favorite mathematics studies. Maria requested and was reassigned to the second shift at Grumman.

She read at home during week-ends, during job lunch breaks and warehouse activity lulls, and during class breaks. Angie was pleased no end that Maria's own *fancy college words* vocabulary grew with each semester. Maria could no longer accuse Angie for using *fancy college words*. However, Maria wanted to be a mathematician, not a pretentious philosopher. But those were the rules. If you wanted a degree, you had to complete 128 credit hours including those hellishly boring courses.

Speaking of hell, how will analyzing *Dante's Inferno* help her earn a living? Maria struggled to regurgitate story minutiae during exams throughout that miserable and useless humanities course. Angie persuaded her to not drop the course. She tutored her, which enabled Maria to eke out a *C* grade. Well, it wasn't a *total* waste of time. At least she earned three more credit hours – three more *miserable* hours!

During her sophomore year Maria took some literature and composition electives. She readily identified with Shakespeare's *Othello*. Maria was the swarthy Moor to Angie's *Desdemona*. She was really pissed when Othello killed the Desdemona chick during a jealous rage. Jealous? Maria thought back to the time Joey's butch sister winked at Angie. *¡Madre mía!* Maria wasn't jealous! She was *possessive*! An idea hit her for a class assignment. She sought Mr. Berski's help to learn the *Dark Eyes* melody structure – eight five-syllable phrases. Simple enough! She titled it *Ode to Dark Eyes*.

> *Dark eyes make it seem*
> *My life's just a dream.*
> *Angels two, I'm blessed,*
> *Huddled to my breast.*
> *Angie gives to me,*
> *Gives her all to me.*
> *Her and Sofie's love*
> *Fit me like a glove.*

Silly? Maybe. But it was structurally correct. So what the hell! It was how she felt! Professor Adler was moved because his Ukraine mother sang the song to him. He told Maria he would disregard her difficulty with homophones and still guarantee her an *A* grade.

"Look! I'm getting an *A* in the course because of this," she exclaimed later that day handing the paper to Angie.

Angie's eyes misted as she read Maria's words. Maria lifted little Sofie onto Angie's lap. "Please sing it to our *angelita*."

Angie honored Maria's request. Little Sofie was too young to understand why her two adults cried. She touched their tears. "Mommy? Auntie?"

*****

Another time Maria participated in a debate topic assignment about the dividing line between American progressives and conservatives on questions of race and justice. Angie's progressive bent greatly influenced Maria. So, of course, she took the progressive side. The opposing side was taken by Jack O'Brien, a pasty-faced classmate. She seethed with anger as he sneered at her while arrogantly presenting the conservative view. She almost rebutted with an *ad hominem* punch to his sickly smarmy smirk. *Damned pendejo paddy!*

Maria's vocabulary expanded such that she could easily speak and think alliteratively – even bilingually.

It was good that other class members held her back preventing a one-on-one Puerto-Rican and Irish rumble right there in the classroom.

Angie got Maria out of the South Bronx but she failed to get the South Bronx out of Maria.

Professor Delgado admired her enthusiasm. Maria signed up for his class because his family was from San Juan. She hoped it would give her a favorite student advantage. It worked!

"Refute the statement. Only the statement," he admonished her.

"Did you see the look he—"

"Only the statement," repeated the professor with a wink. Maria acquiesced.

On the other hand, mathematics was intellectual oxygen – straight A all the way.

There was another time Maria came home after class all excited. "What's going on with you?" asked Angie.

"I just learned the most fantastic thing in statistics."

"What?"

"The central limit theorem."

"Huh?"

"In probability theory, it's a theorem that establishes the normal distribution as—"

"For freaking sake!" interrupted Angie. "I was an English major, so ¡Basta! ¡Ya basta!" Maria doubled over laughing at Angie's attempt at Spanish.

*****

Thus, Maria made it through six sleep-deprived years of consecutive Fall, Spring and Summer semesters to stand at her graduation in cap and gown with Angie and first-grader Sofie.

Six years because as a part-time student she couldn't carry full academic loads and work a full-time second shift at Grumman. Maria's salary supplemented with Angie's widow benefits provided the family a fairly comfortable life. Grumman kept her on after the war during the day, which meant she could only attend evening classes.

Maria hugged Angie while holding her rolled-up diploma. "Thank you, love. Thank you for relentlessly pushing me."

"Well, you did tell me the day we met you were pretty good in math. I wasn't going to let you throw away your talent."

"If he...If Bill hadn't bumped into me I wouldn't be here with the love of my life and her beautiful little girl."

Angie shook her finger at her. "Uh, uh, uh! *Our* beautiful little girl!"

"And to think," said Maria, "I start work next week as a statistician at Professor Mindelman's actuary firm. Imagine that! Jews hiring a *Puertorriqueña*! Who knew?"

"Yeah," said Angie. "New York is a great city!"

1957

Angie, Maria, and Sofie placed flowers on three side-by-side graves with headstones marked:

ISAAC BERSKI/1880-1957
SARAH BERSKI/BELOVED DAUGHTER/
  1909-1909
SOFIA BERSKI/1882-1942

Angie wrapped her arm around her daughter's shoulders. "Uncle Yitzy and his wife loved each other the same wonderful way Daddy and I loved each other."

All were clearly sad, but Sofie was more distraught than her two adults. "I miss him so much, Mom. He baby sat and played with me my whole life. He was so much fun and always made me happy."

"You *also* made him happy," said Angie. "You made up for the baby girl he lost the day she was born."

"You mean I was like a surrogate like Auntie is a surrogate for Daddy?"

The women shot surprised looks at Sofie, then at each other.

"Why the look?" asked Sofie. "You explained that Auntie took Daddy's place as my surrogate parent. Remember?"

They burst with pride that their teen daughter grasped the significance of that word.

"Yes, honey," said Angie, "that's exactly what I mean."
*****

Later that day Angie stood at the high-fidelity system turntable in the living room of their two-bedroom apartment. She hugged the framed wedding portrait to her chest as she gazed trance-like at the spinning record. It was playing *Stardust*.

Maria waited for the song to end. She lifted the tone arm, steered Angie to Sofie's bedroom, and pointed to Sofie. "Half you, half Bill. You never lost all of him."

Mother and daughter embraced with the framed wedding portrait sandwiched between their bodies.

1958

"Sí... Sí, mamá... Estaremos allí... Lo prometo... No... No... Ahora gano mucho dinero. Puedo pagar tu alquiler... Okay! ¡Trato! Mitad del alquiler. Hasta el domingo."

Maria hung up the phone as Angie entered the kitchen. "Here's some official Navy mail for you."

Maria opened the envelope. "Look!" she grinned. "Mateo signed the divorce papers. He's stationed in Vietnam."

"Ooooo!" Angie jested. "I'm no longer living in sin with a married woman."

"That's right! I have even better news. I made partner at my actuary firm. With your chief editor job we can now afford to buy one of those beautiful Manhattan brownstones. I just got off the phone with my folks. We're having dinner there on Sunday. They love their new apartment, especially the elevator. We quibble about letting me pay their rent. They say the 41st Precinct is going to hell."

The apartment door *slammed* shut. The women turned to see Sofie rush past the kitchen door.

Angie called after her. "Honey?"

Sofie's bedroom door *slammed* shut. The women glanced at each other, puzzled. They cautiously opened the bedroom door. Sofie lay face down on her bed, sobbing into her pillow. Her hair and clothing were a bit disheveled. Angie sat on the bed and placed her hand on Sofie's back. "What's wrong, honey?"

"Got into trouble," Sofie mumbled into her pillow.

"Now you turn around, young lady, and tell me what happened. You hear me?"

Sofie turned over. Angie noticed bruises on Sofie's right-hand knuckles.

"I got into a fight. I got into a fight with a boy."

She sat up and hugged her mother.

"I busted his *schnoz*."

"*Schnoz*?"

"Yeah, Mom, *schnoz*! It's a funny word for a nose. I learned it from Uncle Yitzy. It's fun to say *schnoz*. You know, like they call Jimmy Durante *The Schnoz, The Great Schnozzola*."

The two women laughed.

"Anyway, some kids stood around me in the cafeteria listening to this chubby kid laugh and say nasty things, really hurtful things, about you and Auntie. I got madder and madder and he just wouldn't shut up. I lunged at him and knocked him flat on the floor!"

Sofie paused and took a few breaths. "You shoulda seen him there sprawled on the floor scared and holding his bloody *schnoz*."

The women again laughed.

"Anyway, I was gonna kick the shit outa that creep. Oops! Sorry Mom, didn't mean to say that!"

"That's okay, honey. Now go on." Tears dripped down the women's cheeks as they struggled to suppress their laughter.

"Anyway, the teacher-monitor stopped me. She called the nurse who showed up to give him first aid. They hadda take him to the E.R. Mom, he was a bloody mess."

Sofie paused again and took a few breaths. "Then this other boy, in the same class as me, comes right up to me and says, 'Wow! I hope you never get mad at me. I never saw anyone's face seethe with such unbridled rage!'"

Angie was impressed. "Really? Those were his *exact* words?"

"Yeah, that was Hank Richey."

"Same name as ours?"

"No. R-I-C-H-E-Y. He's really smart. Knows lots of neat words. Always gets A-plus on his essays. Wish he would talk to me more. I really like him." *A déjà vu moment for Angie.* "I'll show you how to do that later like Grandma taught me how to get Daddy to talk to me."

"Anyway, that's what happened. Wish the teacher didn't stop me from kicking…ah, nuts!"

The women glanced at each other pinching their lips shut in failed attempts to suppress their laughter.

"You're not gonna think it's so funny. The principal wants you and me to come in to apologize to that kid and his folks."

The women exchanged mischievous glances. *Yeah, like that's going to happen!* They knew how to handle this.

"You're not angry at me?"

"Angry? Honey, Auntie and I thought it impossible to love you more than we already do. You proved us wrong." The women kissed Sofie's bruised knuckles.

*****

Two days later Sofie sat between her two adults at one side of the principal's office. Angie wore a demure dress and Sofie wore typical teen attire. Although Maria was never in a gang, she owned gang-style duds and wore them to this meeting along with fake arm tattoos, exaggerated eye makeup, and tightly pulled-back hair tied into a ponytail. She was one scary-looking Latina!

The women weren't going to let Sofie apologize for defending her adults. So they rehearsed roles for this office visit: Angie, the supportive mother; Maria, the scary intimidator.

Maria glowered at the principal sitting at his desk. *How did she do that without blinking?* Maria's persistent stare made him appear nervous.

Mrs. Jensen, a large haughty woman, and chubby Charlie entered the office. Charlie's face was bruised and bandaged.

Sofie snickered.

"Charlie's father couldn't make it," said Mrs. Jensen.

Sofie bolted out of her chair, rushed toward Charlie, and pointed her finger at him. "At least he still got one," she yelled as he cowered behind his corpulent mother.

Angie's eyes misted over as she pulled Sofie back to her chair.

Maria directed her menacing glower toward Mrs. Jensen and Charlie. She slowly, threateningly, rhythmically tapped her right fist into her left palm. *Blood-chilling message received!* Mrs. Jensen and Charlie dragged their chairs to seat themselves at the other side of the office as far from the Garcia-Ricci trio as possible.

"I asked you here for Sofie to..." the principal nervously glanced at Maria, "...to apologize for starting a fight in the cafeteria two days ago and for injuring Charlie."

Sofie snickered.

Angie wrapped her arm around Sofie's shoulders and narrowed her eyes at the principal. Her response was calm, measured. "That...is not...going...to happen...you pompous ass!"

Everyone in the room was shocked. Angie going off script even caught Maria and Sofie off guard!

Enraged, the principal rose from his seat. Maria glowered, rose from hers, approached, leaned over his desk, and snapped her finger downward. "You catch my drift?" He did! He sat.

Maria returned to her seat and winked at Angie and Sofie. Sofie struggled to keep a straight face.

"You have the unmitigated gall," said Angie, "to demand an apology from my daughter for having her family insulted by that, that little—"

"¡*Mierdita!*" interjected Maria.

"Yeah, that! Miss Garcia and I are Sofie's family—"

"My parents, my parents! Sorry Mom, didn't mean to interrupt."

"Yes, her parents. Sofie was born after her father was, was..." Her eyes welled up. She took some deep breaths. "...was killed in the war. Sofie is a polite young lady, but she won't take any—"

"*¡Mierda!*" again interjected Maria.

"from anyone who insults the two women who raise her." Angie shook her thumb at Charlie.

"Got what he deserved. Yeah, an ass-kicking from a girl!" Angie and Maria each wrapped an arm around Sofie's shoulders. "*Our* girl! We're done here! Let's go!" said Angie.

The Garcia-Ricci trio headed toward the office door.

Mrs. Jensen stood and blocked their way. "You're all going to hell," she expressed sneering at Maria and jabbing Angie's shoulder. "Your lifestyle is sinful and disgusting with someone like that."

¡Madre mía! The physical attack to her angel instantly switched Maria into South Bronx street-fight mode. "*¡Vete al carajo bicha!*" she yelled holding up her fists. Maria glowered and approached the haughty woman. Mrs. Jensen didn't need to know any Spanish to realize that this was turning into a bad day for her – *frightfully bad!*

Angie stopped Maria's approach with her hand. "I'll handle this, love." *The reprehensible insult to her devoted companion eclipsed the shoulder jab.* Angie's face flushed, her lips curled, and seething hatred emanated from her normally comforting dark eyes.

Maria was not one easily frightened, but this time she crossed herself as her sweet angel's reddening face morphed into...into...*¡Madre mía!*...into *¡El Diablo!* And yet her petite angel staring down that massive Mrs. Jensen did make a comical *David and Goliath* scene – female version. But just in case, Maria was the always ready backup – just in case.

Sofie gripped Maria's other hand. She had never ever seen that look on her mother.

Angie glowered at the large woman and pointed to Maria with her other hand. "Someone like *that*? Someone like *that*? You *hateful* racist bitch! How *dare* you!" Angie back-hand slapped Mrs. Jensen's face, knocking her into Charlie, and crashing them unceremoniously onto her seat.

Sofie and Maria laughed out loud at the comical scene. Well, comical for them – not so much for the Jensens.

Failing to see the humor, the principal rose from his seat. Maria instantly darted her frightening glower at him. Once again she pointed and snapped down her finger. And once again he meekly sat back down.

Maria hugged Angie. "*¡Amo, amo, te amo tanto!*" She shook her fist and glowered at the very terrified Mrs. Jensen.

Sofie clapped her hands and gazed with awestruck pride at her two adults. The principal and the Jensens were stunned into shocked silence. Angie gripped Maria and Sofie's hands and they stormed out of the office into the hallway.

*****

Sofie held Angie and Maria's hands as they approached the school main entrance. She kissed Angie's cheek, turned to Maria, and kissed her cheek. "What was that Spanish you yelled at Charlie's mom?"

"Not gonna say. It's bad! Really bad!"

"Really *that* bad?"

"Oh yeah! Don't *ever* say it in your Spanish class or to any Spanish speakers. Not even as a joke. You hear me?"

"Okay, okay, I won't! Anyway, Mom's a badass like you."

"Runs in the family, *angelita*. I'll bet word gets around at school to never mess with the Ricci *chica*."

"Ricci *chica*. Ricci *chica*. Ricci *chica*," laughed Sofie. "It sounds like a choo-choo train. *Woo! Woo!* It's fun to say Ricci *chica*."

"Fun like *schnoz*?" asked Angie.

"Yeah, Mom, fun like *schnoz*."

Oh, the joy Sofie brought to their lives! Bursting with pride, the two women glanced at each other, then at their daughter.

1959

The family had moved into their newly renovated central air conditioned Manhattan brownstone townhouse during the year. The adults watched with pride as Sofie mounted the *GARCIA RICCI* doorbell nameplate. Sofie later mounted the Gold Star banner in one of the front windows to honor her father's sacrifice.

Sofie sat at her small desk one Sunday afternoon. Several closed schoolbooks and the framed wedding portrait of her parents were on the desk. Angie stood in the doorway. "How's your homework assignment coming along, honey?"

Sofie smiled at her. "Just finished it."

Her smile faded as she gazed at the framed portrait. Mother and daughter gazed at the portrait together. Angie briefly left the room and returned with a lipstick stained V-mail letter wrinkled with dried tears.

"These are Daddy's last loving words to me. He missed me very much and was happy and relieved I found a roommate."

Sofie read the letter and pointed to a sentence about making a baby. "Yes, honey. I didn't know when I wrote Daddy that I was pregnant with you."

"Tell me all about the last time you saw Daddy."

A silent moment passed. Angie grasped Sofie's hand. "Come!"

*****

Angie hailed a taxi. "Penn Station 7th Avenue entrance, please," she instructed the driver.

*****

The cavernous concourse was almost deserted. A small crowd milled about.

Angie pointed toward the stairs to tracks three and four. "There! That's where I saw Daddy for the last time. We threw kisses to each other. I waved until Daddy disappeared into the gate."

Angie gazed down the stairs, reliving the moment in her mind. Tears dripped down her cheeks. "There, on Sunday July fifth nineteen forty two, two-thirty-two in the afternoon."

She clutched her clenched fists to her chest, *gasped*, *wailed*.

"B I I I I I I I LL!!!!"

Bill's name echoed in the cavernous space. Angie's legs buckled. Sofie grabbed her and they collapsed to their knees. Sofie helped her mother to stand, steered her to the benches, caressed, and calmed her.

"Honey, do you *really* wanna know *all* about the last time I saw Daddy?"

"Yes, Mom. Everything. Please. Everything."

"Okay then," said Angie taking a deep breath. "I'm going to tell you something parents rarely tell their kids." Angie grasped Sofie's hand. "Come!"

*****

They stood in the restroom area corridor. Angie pointed to the men's room door. "Daddy gave me his last gift in there. My most precious gift."

Angie caressed and kissed her daughter. "The beautiful gift that gave me you."

1966

Sofie danced with her husband at their wedding reception. Angie and Maria were overwhelmed with joy. "She looks as beautiful as you did the day we met," said Maria.

Despite the joy of that day and the joy Maria brought to her life, Angie could not dispel her lingering sorrow that Bill could not be there to see the beautiful child they had created.

"My baby is now Mrs. Henry Richey. She met her guy just like I met Bill. Yeah, as they say, like mother, like daughter."

The band played *Stardust*. Angie's eyes welled up. She fidgeted with her wedding band and closed her eyes. Visions of what might have been paraded through her mind.

Little Sofie runs to Bill as he exits Penn Station gate with a seabag over his shoulder.

Bill reads a bedtime story to his little Sofie.

Angie and Bill sit on a park bench exchanging loving glances as they watch first grader Sofie in the playground.

Angie, preteen Sofie and Bill laugh as they watch a funny movie.

Bill helps Sofie with her high school homework.

Sofie, in cap and gown, hugs and kisses Angie and Bill at her college graduation.

Bride Sofie dances with Bill. She hugs and kisses him.

Maria intuitively knew what was going through her best friend's mind. She removed a handkerchief from her evening clutch and wiped Angie's tears.

1967

Maria was unable to calm Angie as she anxiously paced back and forth in the hospital maternity waiting room. Hank's folks had not yet arrived.

"Why the hell doesn't somebody tell us what's going on," complained Angie as she nervously glanced at the wall clock – 2:30. "It's been almost two hours since my baby was taken to the delivery room."

Angie continued pacing. She again glanced at the clock – 2:32. *Oh no!* Anxiety about her daughter and suddenly recalling the moment she last saw Bill at Penn Station exacerbated her state of mind. "Bill, Bill," she murmured. Tears of sadness dripped down her cheeks as she collapsed onto a chair.

Maria, ever ready to comfort her angel, caressed her.

At that precise 2:32 moment, Hank rushed into the waiting room and grasped Angie's hands. "It's a boy, Mom, a healthy little boy," he said bursting with fatherly pride. Angie's sad tears became tears of joy.

"Come!" Hank beckoned. Angie and Maria followed him to the recovery room where Sofie sat in bed cradling her son in her arms.

"Here, Mom," said Sofie. "Hold your grandson. We named him after Daddy."

Sofie and Maria held hands. They shared Angie's profound joy as she caressed and kissed her little Bill.

THE END

APPENDIX

Angie & Maria is a story about a devoted friendship that began during World War II and continued to the post-war years. The fictionalized story is based upon actual places and events illustrated in this appendix.

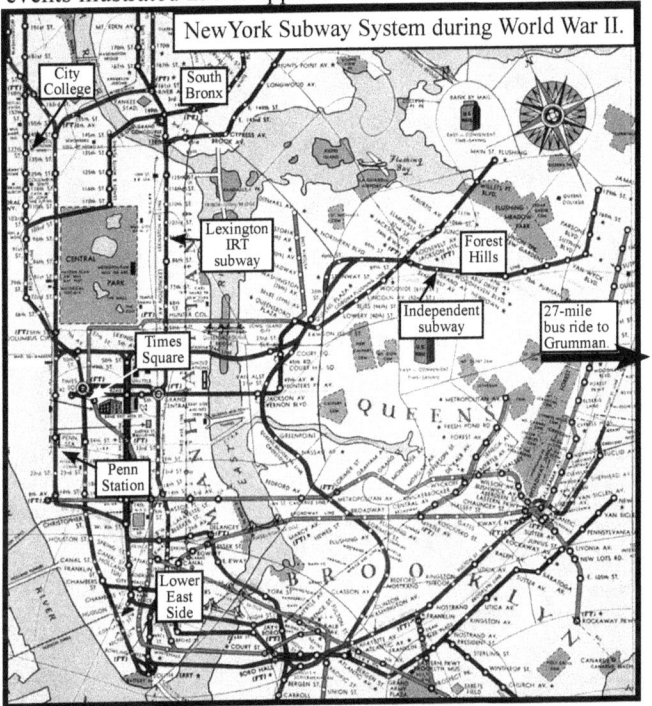

New York Subway System during World War II.

City College · South Bronx · Lexington IRT subway · Forest Hills · Independent subway · 27-mile bus ride to Grumman · Times Square · Penn Station · Lower East Side

Grumman F6F Hellcat factory in Bethpage where Angie and Maria worked during the war.

Original 1910 Penn Station 7th Avenue entrance.

Angie and Maria stood across the street when Penn Station demolition commenced on October 28, 1963.

Penn Station demolition scenes.

Angie and Maria first met in the Penn Station concourse then later learned about each other in a typical Automat restaurant like this.

Angie looked at the clock after Bill entered the gate to track 3. The time was 2:32 p.m.

Angie and Bill's farewell caress.

Stairs to track 3 where Angie last saw Bill.

Seabees at work on Guadalcanal where Bill was assigned.

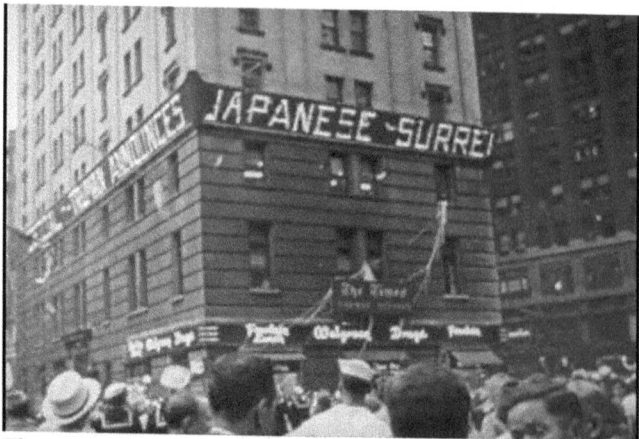

The marquee on the New York Times building in Times Square announced the end of World War II on August 14, 1945. It was here in August 1942 Angie learned that Seabees joined up with Marines on Guadalcanal.

Angie and Maria visited Penn Station for one last time before demolition commenced.

Maria began her final move away from the South Bronx on the IRT subway line then transferred to the Independent line to Queens-Forest Hills (inset).

Maria moved to Angie's new Queens apartment from a deteriorating South Bronx tenement.

The Garcia-Ricci family moved into their brownstone townhouse in 1959.

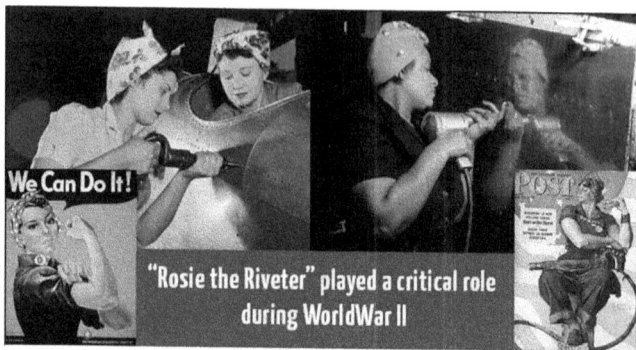

Angie and Maria were also World War II *Rosies*. They worked at Grumman to produce F6F Hellcat carrier-based fighters. Angie worked the day shift. Maria worked the 2nd shift so she could attend City College day classes to earn her mathematics degree.

Daycare centers were provided for working mothers, which enabled Angie to return to work after giving birth to Sofie.

Thousands of women workers were laid off after the war.

Maria was kept on as a mathematician in the engineering department during the day – attended evening classes to complete her degree. She left in 1948 to join a New York actuary firm as a statistician.

Angie found work in the burgeoning New York publishing industry where she quickly advanced to chief editor.

1940s New York neighborhood candy store.

Egg cream contains neither cream nor egg. Carbonated water squirted into chocolate syrup and milk makes a foam topping.

1940s New York neighborhood grocery.

www.ingramcontent.com/pod-product-compliance
Lightning Source LLC
Chambersburg PA
CBHW071137280326
41935CB00010B/1262